PARIS

By Rudolph Chelminski
and the Editors of Time-Life Books

Photographs by Raghubir Singh

THE GREAT CITIES · TIME-LIFE BOOKS · AMSTERDAM

The Author: Born in Wilton, Connecticut, Rudolph Chelminski graduated from Harvard University in 1956. After U.S. Army service in Korea and a stint as a journalist in Denver, Colorado, he went to Paris in 1961 on a year's fellowship from the French government. He returned there the following year as a correspondent for LIFE Magazine. Except for two years as LIFE's Moscow bureau chief, Paris has been his home ever since. Now a freelance, he is the author of many articles and a non-fiction book, *Prisoner of Mao*.

The Photographer: Raghubir Singh was born in Jaipur, India, in 1942. Since 1966 his work has been published in magazines around the world. He has also produced two books — *Ganga: Sacred River of India* and *Calcutta*.

THE GREAT CITIES
EDITOR: Dale Brown
Design Consultant: Louis Klein
Picture Editor: Pamela Marke
Assistant Picture Editor: Anne Angus

Editorial Staff for Paris
Text Editors: John Cottrell, Jim Hicks
Designer: Graham Davis
Staff Writers: Mike Brown, Deborah Thompson
Text Researchers: Susan Dawson, Susan Goldblatt, Vanessa Kramer, Elizabeth Loving
Design Assistant: Shirin Patel

Editorial Production for the Series
Art Department: Julia West
Editorial Department: Ellen Brush, Betty H. Weatherley
Picture Department: Thelma Gilbert, Christine Hinze

The captions and text of the picture essays were written by the staff of TIME-LIFE Books.

Valuable assistance was given in the preparation of this volume by TIME-LIFE Correspondents Maria Vincenza Aloisi and Joséphine du Brusle.

Cover: Viewed from a perspective beneath its familiar splayed legs, foreshortened against the sky, Paris' most famous landmark, the Eiffel Tower, assumes an entirely new geometry.

First end paper: Etched in the glass door of the famed Crazy Horse Saloon, the figure of a sleekly winsome siren promises customers as they enter that Paris will live up to its international reputation for sexy and sophisticated nightlife.

Last end paper: Its paint peeling, the wall of a Paris laundry advertises the establishment with this scene picturing a working girl in clogs hanging up washing.

Published by TIME-LIFE International (Nederland) B.V. Ottho Heldringstraat 5, Amsterdam 1018.

© 1977 TIME-LIFE International (Nederland) B.V. All rights reserved.

To Norman,

That reluctant student of
the French language.

With love from,

Ken & Suzanne.

Contents

I

Indomitable Paris

Now that I look back, I realize that I had the luck to encounter Paris five or six days before I had ever set foot there. The time was the early Sixties; the place was the Atlantic Ocean, aboard *Flandre*, a little ship of the Compagnie Générale Transatlantique; and, as one of many American students in Tourist Class, I was *en voyage* to a year at l'Institut d'Études Politiques, thanks to a fellowship granted by the French government.

My seagoing introduction to Paris began with the food. Even in the Tourist Class dining room, we ate like visiting gentry—plied with as much first-rate French cooking as we could force down our near-insatiable gullets, and given free wine as well. Relaxed but gracious presentation made the meals the high points of our days. As the French always have known, and as I was just beginning to learn, it is at the table that humankind is most civilized, conversation brightest, optimism most accessible.

The uncontested star and leader of our table was an 80-year-old gentleman from New Orleans—a renegade Parisian, dapper, energetic and charming. He had emigrated from Paris more than half a century earlier, and yet he spoke of the city as though he had been away only for a long weekend. That, I came to learn, is typical of Paris and Parisians: the city marks its children for life.

Our elderly friend dominated the table with his effortless grace and wit, regaling us with reminiscences and advice, and enjoying the sound of his own voice as much as we did. The French—and especially the Parisians, the women as much as the men—are bred to talk. When they do it badly, they are interminable bores. When they do it well—and most of them do—they are superbly entertaining.

If a Parisian seems to talk too much (as some Americans, less voluble by nature, have complained to me), it does not necessarily mean that he is an attention-seeking egotist. He has been taught to talk, as a social responsibility. The Anglo-Saxon respects words for their literal meaning, the Frenchman for their decorative effect as well, for the filigrees of *bons mots* he can spin in the air. If an Englishman or a German says something outrageous, chances are that he believes it. If a Frenchman says something outrageous, and he almost always does, there is little cause for alarm. In time, you can be virtually certain, he will be saying the opposite.

The *Flandre* also introduced me to the most Parisian of odours: the rich, acrid and intoxicating smoke of Gauloises, the characteristic French cigarette. Today still, the smell of Gauloises is as pervasively Parisian as low-octane gasoline is a reminder to me of Moscow, where I once lived.

In the doorway of an apartment house, a redoubtable Parisian concierge (caretaker) relaxes without losing that look of sharp-eyed inquisitiveness that all lodgers learn to respect. The concierge, a Paris institution since Napoleon's reign, has come to embody the self-assured attitude of the typical Parisian.

I took to Gauloises as soon as I came aboard ship (they cost one-third the price of American cigarettes), and even now, when I have been off smoking for years, the strong, mellow taste of that black tobacco haunts me like a Proustian *madeleine* multiplied by ten. The advantage of Gauloises addiction, though, is that once you have quit smoking there is little chance you will become a backslider. After them, everything else seems bland, feeble and uninteresting. It took me rather longer to become accustomed to the strange, bright-yellow aniseed aperitif that the French passengers invariably took before meals. In truth, *pastis* is traditionally associated with the South of France, but its tongue-numbing liquorice taste is as typical of Paris as the taste of Scotch whisky is of London.

Most of all, I learned about Paris from the ship's crew, especially the dining-room personnel who amazed me with their intelligence and humour and gaiety. Unlike most of their brethren around the world, French waiters actually *enjoy* their work. And beyond the dining room, I found that the crew led a double life: keeping the ship functioning while unabashedly involving themselves with the passengers. A deckhand could always spare five minutes from his brass-polishing to have a chat, usually instigated by himself, and officers accepted such breaches of marine etiquette with affable equanimity. Discipline was a bore, deadening to the spirit.

One evening a steward suggested that if I and a group of my friends felt like breaking the monotony, we could always go and see what the swells were doing up in First Class. "But is that allowed?" one of us asked naïvely. "Allowed?" The steward raised an eyebrow, shrugged, and expelled a puff of breath to create the sound that is more representative of the Parisian mentality than the *Marseillaise: "Bof!"*

"*Vas-y, mon petit.* Go ahead," he said. "No one will stop you." And he was right. No one paid the slightest attention to our wanderings through the ship. Indeed, the First Class passengers were delighted to see us. They were bored up there, in their expensive dresses and tuxedos.

Some years later—after living in Paris for a while—I made the mistake of trying the same transgression aboard the old *Queen Elizabeth.* I was stopped cold in my tracks and escorted back to Tourist Class—a trespasser in deepest disgrace. On an objective level I clearly deserved it; I had been creeping about, putting my nose where it didn't belong, hoping to find and partake of privileges for which I hadn't paid. What it proved was that I had become a Parisian in spirit. Such rude and self-indulgent behaviour is typically, quintessentially French and, *a fortiori*, Parisian. It is predicated on an ancient racial wisdom about balancing humanity versus authority. Life is too short and potentially enjoyable, human intercourse too beautiful and too complex to be governed by a dour set of absolutes that brook no bendings or exceptions. No one in the world is more amenable to argument and exception than a Parisian ("*Bof! Vas-y, mon petit.* Just don't tell the boss I let you through.")

Three determined spectators at a Bastille Day parade peer through cardboard periscopes—one decorated with Paris scenes—in order to see over the crowd. Every July 14, a national holiday, Paris erupts in festivities to commemorate the fall of the notorious prison, the Bastille, during the revolution of 1789.

A few years back an eccentric French lady of my acquaintance once passed on to me a neat little formula she had picked up on her travels:

In England, everything is allowed except what is forbidden;

In Germany, everything is forbidden, except what is allowed;

In Russia, everything is forbidden, even what is allowed;

In France, everything is allowed, even what is forbidden.

Now I can't affirm this as the final distillate of the truth about Paris and the aggravating, complicated, subtle and talented people who inhabit it. But it comes close enough.

My fast-developing prejudice in favour of the French was fortified by my first encounter with their officialdom. On the boat train from Le Havre to Paris' Gare St-Lazare, the police had made only a cursory check on our passports—but Customs promised to be a trial. After all, the other students and I were travelling with as much clothing and equipment as we would need for a year; I was even carrying a 40-pound typewriter at the bottom of my duffel bag. When the Customs officer appeared, we scarcely had a chance to open our mouths. "*Étudiants?*" cried the face below the peaked cap. "*Oui,*" we chorused, making ready to mumble our declarations in our schoolboy French. But already he was gone. Welcome to France, I thought. This is a no-problem country. And I was right.

I was lucky to be travelling with my old friend Chuck Krance, later to become a professor of French literature in the United States. Chuck knew Paris well and, as a result, my first vision of the capital—the one that will always stick in my mind's eye as the symbol of the city—was old Place St-Sulpice, just around the corner from St-Germain des Prés. We took a taxi there from St-Lazare station, and on the way I saw only a jumble of shops and sooty-fronted buildings. But then suddenly everything changed when we turned down Rue de Vieux Colombier and into Place St-Sulpice. It was like driving into a Monet canvas. Imposing stands of red chestnuts, their leaves just browning and beginning to fall, filtered the autumn sunlight that dappled over white gravel and green benches, where children played noisily and pensioners leaned forward on canes watching silently. In the centre of the square, Lodovico Visconti's huge fountain, dedicated to four famous bishops, accentuated the verdant and shady secrecy of the little park with its soot-blackened stonework and barely rippling water. Everything about St-Sulpice was calm, reserved, umbrageous—an immensely appealing withdrawal from the 20th-Century racket and commerce on near-by Rue de Rennes, Rue du Four and St-Germain.

Directly ahead, through and above the treetops, loomed the ponderous and preposterous façade of St-Sulpice itself, one of the world's strangest churches. In a land that boasts an incomparable wealth of exquisite ecclesiastical architecture of all styles, St-Sulpice stands out as a bizarre and most ungainly sore thumb—the disastrous outcome of too many architects commissioned over too great a span of time—six in all, over a period of 134 years. The stone-cutting and workmanship are admirable enough, but the massive pillared façade, the two disjointed and asymmetrical towers and the Jesuit-style main body sit in heavy opposition to one another. Jet-black as it was then (as was all of Paris before Minister of Cultural Affairs André Malraux's great clean-up campaign in the 1960s), it seemed the entrance to night, blocking off an entire side of the *place*.

At the south-east corner of the square, stuck off behind a little continuation of the park—with its own few chestnut trees, its own few benches —was the tiny Hôtel Récamier, where Chuck had reserved a room for himself and his wife. The Récamier was so like a Hollywood movie set I would not have been surprised to see Gene Kelly leap out of the front door, sail over a bench and go dancing down Rue des Canettes. The narrow, high-shouldered building was only six storeys tall and only two windows wide. Its 30 small rooms could be reached by means of a delicate glass-and-mahogany box that shook and rumbled upwards inside the coil of the spiral staircase. It was forbidden to use the lift for descent. After all, the staff argued with impeccable Cartesian logic, an elevator by its very name was meant to elevate, not to lower.

The "staff", in this instance, was one white-haired and rather suspicious old lady. It did not take us long to understand that the real reason for the one-way elevator was to save wear and tear on the machinery. The French have a passion for saving, for conserving, for squeezing every last and conceivable bit of utility out of anything in which they have invested time or money. (Remember Guy de Maupassant's *A Piece of String*?) And for me this was indelibly illustrated at the Récamier by my introduction to that most French of all inventions, *la minuterie*.

You see them all over France—on every landing of every apartment house, hotel or office building: little buttons in the wall, often phosphorescent to make them more visible in the dark; when pushed, they give you exactly one minute of light. One minute in principle, that is. In reality, it is not unusual to encounter maniac *minuteries* whose timing mechanisms have become deranged with age (or have been tampered with by white-haired women fiendishly intent on creating "*seconderies*") and which barely let you down one flight of stairs before the light winks out, forcing you to grope along the wall for the next button. In these tricky situations, the chances are about 50-50 that you will hit someone's door-bell instead of the next *minuterie*, so that your descent to the next landing is accompanied by muffled cries of "*Qui est là?*"

The Récamier, I am happy to say, is still there, cowering in its corner in the lee of St-Sulpice, and the lift is still exclusively a lift. But the tall chestnuts have gone from the square. They were chopped down a few years back when progress, in the form of an underground parking garage, came to this tranquil backwater of the Left Bank. The Paris Parks Service did their best to restore the *place* after digging it up. Visconti's monumental fountain, with its four seated bishops, is back in the middle, and you can hardly detect the lines where workers cut it up when they carted it away for safekeeping while the subterranean digging went on. Unfortunately, the new chestnuts that were subsequently planted around the fountain are still young, providing inadequate shade and only symbolic greenery against the aggressive brilliance of white gravel underfoot and the newly cleaned stonework of the church.

Leaving the Krances to settle into the Récamier, I set out in search of a hotel for myself. But all sense of urgency was immediately lost. It was one of those glorious autumn days. With all deference to Tin Pan Alley, September and October in Paris are the best months; April is usually terrible, chilly and rainy. The air in the autumn is warm yet fresh, the light subtler than in midsummer, the winter rains around the corner. As I struck out across the square and down through the little lanes leading out towards Boulevard St-Germain, I was stopped in my tracks again and again. Everything was strange, funny, exciting: so many overhanging, crazily out-of-plumb 17th-Century buildings; a brazenly striped tabby perched between two lofty geranium pots and gazing down on me with infinite superiority; the cockeyed parade of unexpected shop fronts— brooms and baskets hanging from the ceiling in this one, fat loaves of country bread in the next, a dimly lit bar inside another where the Auvergnat proprietor dispensed wine on the zinc counter and sold sacks of charcoal and kindling wood from the storeroom behind. What a city!

My aimless stroll took me across Boulevard St-Germain and down Rue de Buci to its intersection with Rue de Seine. There I had my first plunge into that garden of delights for eye, nose and palate: the Buci open-air market. Paris has taught me many things, but one of the most useful is that the best way to know a people is through its food markets. In Beirut or Barcelona or Bari (all great market towns), go where the locals are buying their fish, oranges and garlic and you will be better instructed about the population than in all their best museums. Latins are public people; in the street everyone is part performer and part spectator. The market is the forum where the show of life goes on, and nowhere is the show better than in the Marché Buci.

Into the milling, swirling crowds poured the voices of the stallholders who vie with each other in France, as they do in Italy, for volume and speed of delivery and the colourful image given at just the right moment. "Take a little look, take a little look, take a little look," chanted a courgette-seller *basso continuo*, as his colleague, high tenor, counterpointed with brilliant improvisations about his *frisée* lettuces. "Two francs for three, two francs for three," someone else sang with breathless urgency, while a fish vendor latched on to a pretty, young pregnant woman and strongly

MONTMARTRE

Rue Caulaincourt

●**Moulin Rouge**

PIGALLE

Parc Monceau

●**Gare St-Lazare**

Place Charles de Gaulle
(ex Place de l'Étoile)

Arc de Triomphe

Avenue Franklin D. Roosevelt

Champs-Elysées

●**Élysée
Palace**

Opéra

Avenue Victor Hugo

La Madeleine *Boulevard
des Capucines*

*Place
Vendôme*

Avenue de l'Opéra

Grand Palais ●

●**Petit Palais**

Rue Royale

**Colonne
d'Austerlitz**

**Obélisque
de Luxor**

*Place de
la Concorde*

Rue de Rivoli

**Palais de
Chaillot**

*Pont
Alexandre III*

Tuileries Gardens

RIVER SEINE

**Arc de Triomphe
du Carrousel**

Louvre●

Eiffel Tower

*Pont du
Carrousel*

*Pont
des Arts*

*Square du
Vert-Galant*

Rue de Grenelle

Boulevard St-Germain

**St. Germain-
des-Prés**

Champ-de-Mars

●**Hôtel des Invalides**

Rue de Grenelle

Rue de Varenne

Rue de Seine

Église du Dôme

Boulevard Raspail

●**École Militaire**

LEFT BANK

St-Sulpice

*Place
de l'Odéon*

U.N.E.S.C.O

Rue de Rennes

Luxembourg Gardens

Boulevard du Montparnasse

Boulevard St-Michel

MONTPARNASSE

Avenue de l'Observatoire

Boulevard Raspail

*Montparnasse
Cemetery*

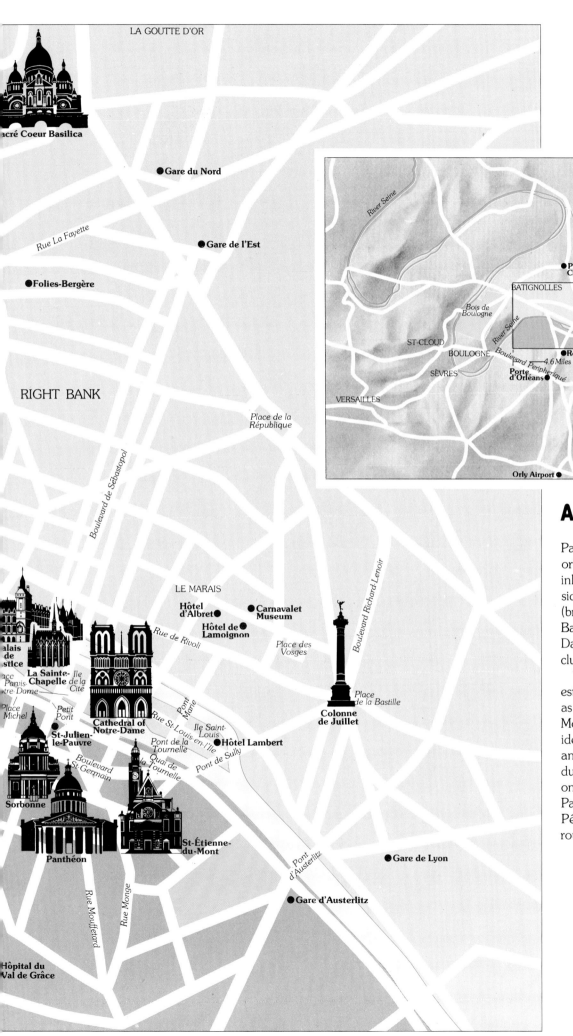

LA GOUTTE D'OR

Sacré Coeur Basilica

● Gare du Nord

Rue La Fayette

● Gare de l'Est

● Folies-Bergère

RIGHT BANK

*Place de la
République*

Boulevard de Sébastopol

River Seine

● Basilica of St-Denis

Canal St-Denis

Canal de l'Ourcq

● Porte de
Clignancourt

BATIGNOLLES

*Parc des
Buttes-Chaumont*

BELLEVILLE

*Bois de
Boulogne*

CHARONNE

St-Germain-
de-Charonne ●

● Porte de
Montreuil

ST-CLOUD

River Seine

River Marne

BOULOGNE

Boulevard Périphérique

● Royal Observatory

*Bois de
Vincennes*

SÈVRES

4.6 Miles

VERSAILLES

Porte
d'Orléans ●

● Porte
d'Italie

Orly Airport ●

LE MARAIS

Hôtel
d'Albret ●

● Carnavalet
Museum

Hôtel de
Lamoignon ●

Rue de Rivoli

*Place des
Vosges*

Colonne
de Juillet

Boulevard Richard Lenoir

*Place
de la Bastille*

Palais
de
Justice

La Sainte-
Chapelle

*Place
Parvis-
Notre-Dame*

*Île
de la
Cité*

Place
St Michel

*Petit
Pont*

Cathedral of
Notre-Dame

*Pont
Marie*

St-Julien-
le-Pauvre

*Rue St-Louis
en-l'Île*

*Île Saint-
Louis*

● Hôtel Lambert

*Pont de la
Tournelle*

*Boulevard
St-Germain*

*Quai de
la Tournelle*

Pont de Sully

Sorbonne

Panthéon

St-Étienne-
du-Mont

Rue Mouffetard

Rue Monge

*Pont
d'Austerlitz*

● Gare de Lyon

● Gare d'Austerlitz

Hôpital du
Val de Grâce

A Monumental Metropolis

Paris grew outwards from the Île de la Cité—
originally the stronghold of its namesake
inhabitants, the Parisii—to spread over both
sides of the sinuous Seine: the Left Bank
(brown on the map at left) and the Right
Bank (cream). Early buildings like Notre-
Dame, La Sainte-Chapelle and the Louvre
cluster on and around this island heart.

The expanding city swallowed up smaller
established communities, but some—such
as St-Germain des Prés, Montmartre and
Montparnasse—maintained their distinct
identities. These and the broad boulevards
and parks laid out in the 19th Century
during replanning of the city are featured
on the large map. Today the old city of
Paris, within the ring of its Boulevard
Périphérique (small map above), is surrounded by a sprawl of modern suburbs.

advised her to buy a fillet of sole for the future good of her impending offspring, promising that if she did so she would produce a son almost as handsome as he.

The Buci had three fish stalls (one has since been replaced by a dry goods emporium) within the space of a city block; and ranged between them were a couple of butchers, one *boucherie chevaline* (selling fresh horse-meat and its conserved derivatives), two enormous vegetable stands, two cheese shops, two *épiceries* (French versions of grocery shops that make the American ones look like Mother Hubbard's cupboard), a *triperie* (the tripe specialists my wife refers to as "offal organ grinders") and a variety of smaller stands.

In the cacophony of the market, only the two cheese ladies (curiously, cheese is almost always sold by ladies of dignified, reserved comportment) remained silent. They sat in their white smocks, peering over Crottins de Chavignol *fromage frais*, bottles of milk, baskets brimful with eggs, and high, yellow mounds of fresh butter that they neatly sliced up with a wire held taut between two wooden handles.

What a city! I sat at a café's sidewalk table and nursed a beer for half an hour, watching the show. On a corner a jocular old man in a blue blouse was hawking beautifully fresh, real coconut macaroons; near by, a straggle-haired, middle-aged hippie was carrying on a monologue from his bicycle in a vain effort to sell his outrageous, surrealistic newspaper (*La Presse Périodique*); and across the way some intensely serious Communist and socialist youths were marching up and down among the shoppers, brandishing *Lutte Ouvrière*, *l'Humanité* and *Unité*, Communist and socialist papers, and entreating everyone present to remain vigilant against the encroachments of devil capitalism and to support the just struggle of the workers against the bosses, against the de Gaulle government and against the entire Western economic system.

Since that first visit, I have been back to the Buci a thousand times. I can still sit there happily for hours, watching the French at their Frenchest. Nowadays, however, I make it a policy not to go there hungry; otherwise I will return home laden with more food than my family and I can hope to devour. In America, the supermarket geniuses invented the science of packaging to make items sell. In France, they have an even cleverer marketing trick: they display the produce fresh, without any packaging.

As I sat with my beer, I looked up and noticed that the very bar I was patronizing had a small hotel attached. "Bar-Hôtel Stella Artois", the big sign said. How convenient. Within minutes I found myself signed up for a room at the ridiculously low cost of ten francs. I ambled back to St-Sulpice to tell Chuck and his wife Mary Ann that I would be staying at the Hôtel Stella Artois. Chuck raised a speculative eyebrow. "Are you sure that's the name?" "Why, yes," I said. "The Bar-Hôtel Stella Artois." Patiently, Chuck explained that Stella Artois was the name of a brand of Belgian beer. Any

A flower seller in the Passy quarter on Paris' Right Bank continues her sales talk to a critical-looking customer even as she hands him a bunch of fresh tulips from her barrow. She is one of many such flower vendors who are found all over Paris and add splashes of brilliant colour to the city's busy streets.

bar or restaurant that contracted to sell it on draught would receive, as a free sales bonus, a handsome, hand-painted sign. My announcement had been roughly equivalent to a Frenchman arriving in Indianapolis and telling friends he was staying at the Coca-Cola Hotel.

The "Stella Artois" (I never did discover its real name) gave me my second lesson of the day in French mechanical accessories. This time it was the door buzzer. The side entrance leading up to my room had an electric lock that freed the door at the push of a button set in the wall. The button also activated a clamorous buzzer next to the cashier's desk, where Madame could look up from her accounts, see me walk in and ascertain whether I was alone. Not that she cared for any moral reasons; what concerned her was that an extra person should pay an extra charge. This ubiquitous buzzer—every front door of every apartment house in Paris opens with one—is a direct descendant of the Napoleonic institution of the *concierge*, that omniscient sentinel who, in days before electricity or gas, used to unbolt the main entrance and, candle in hand, guide apartment dwellers to their doors—a role the *concierge* neatly combined with that of police and tax informer. With modernization, the buzzer has supplanted the iron knocker and bell, and the *minuterie* has replaced the candle. But the *concierges* remain, usually relegated to mean little cold-water, one-room apartments on the ground floor, opposite the stairway. Through their glass doors they see everything, know everything. It is an excellent idea to stay on the right side of your *concierge*.

I didn't achieve much academically at l'Institut d'Études Politiques that year. In fact, one might say I downright squandered my fellowship. But I prefer to think that I re-routed it—redistributing its benefits from scholarship to walking, looking and talking. I learned Paris. Eventually I moved out of my perch above the Stella Artois bar and settled into the Luxembourg, a sombre but relatively clean student hotel on Rue Royer-Collard, uphill from the Sorbonne. Twice a day, with the predictability of a tide, I was drawn towards the miraculously cheap (one franc a meal) student restaurant down on Rue de Médicis. The remainder of my time was given less to lectures and study than to exploration: roaming through the twisting maze of medieval streets behind the Panthéon, down Boul' Mich into the even more ancient St-Séverin quarter, over to Montparnasse and St-Germain des Prés, and sometimes into the more glamorous Seventh Arrondissement (for administrative purposes Paris is divided into 20 *arrondissements* or districts) with its trio of landmarks: the Hôtel des Invalides, the École Militaire and the Eiffel Tower.

On very rare occasions I even ventured out among the tourists and merchant philistines of the Right Bank, all the time buttressing my failing resolve—enemy territory!—with the fine-honed contempt that only a poor student can feel for the other side of the river: the wealthy, industrious,

In spite of grim weather, Paris begins a spectacular Bastille Day celebration with a fly-past of jets trailing smoke plumes of red, white and blue—the colours of the French flag. In the foreground police keep the Champs-Élysées clear for a military parade —barely visible in the rainy distance— approaching from the Arc de Triomphe.

bourgeois side. I had a somewhat artificially developed scorn for Hemingway, Fitzgerald and other semi-mythic American literary figures who had larked over to Paris 40 or so years before me, most of them without bothering to learn the language but instead settling into arty, Anglo-Saxon ghettos typified by the Hôtel Ritz on Place Vendôme and Harry's American Bar at 5 Rue Daunou. Harry's Bar indeed! *Sank roo doenoo*, indeed! As for Hemingway's celebrated wartime stunt of "liberating" the Ritz Bar by being the first to arrive there when the Allies entered Paris, that was about as swashbuckling as a safari in a Rolls-Royce. Bah! We purists would rather have swallowed gall than set foot in the Ritz Bar.

On those obsessional promenades I kept an indispensable notebook, jotting down French phrases and words that *seem* simple enough now, but that *were* utterly bedevilling then. Th labours of trying to replace "get"— that fabulous, all-purpose English verb—in my French conversation gave me months of frustration, during which advice from my 80-year-old friend aboard *Flandre* kept coming back to me. "It is futile to try to make the French language behave like English. The only way to make it work is to start thinking like a Frenchman." His advice applied equally well to the country as a whole—and especially to its capital. I certainly think in French now; I even have a Parisian accent on top of my American one so that when I go to the provinces I am instantly identified as an American from Paris. But do I think like a Parisian? After all these years, I would say "yes"—to a large degree, at any rate.

Without doubt, the Parisian is different from the rest of the French. As millions of tourists discover every summer, he is not the sort who inspires instant affection. The Parisian is quick, impatient, difficult, sceptical, unsentimental, sarcastic—and very smart. While I would be happy to claim these virtues for myself, I'm afraid the best I can do is admire them and sometimes reflect them, as I did when I trespassed aboard *Queen Elizabeth*, shamelessly seeking personal gain in violation of the rules of the collective. That incident might well be taken as a microcosm of the Parisian attitude that is just one blink this side of anarchy. A rebel at heart, the Parisian has never quite accepted the lines of authority of the ship of state. He believes himself to be just as smart as the prince or the rich bourgeois above him—and he usually is. So how come they are up there and he down here? The answer, his reason tells him, is simple: because they got into a position of power and then made the rules. Consequently, the individual who spends his life passively obeying the rules is a *couillon*— a dope (or worse). Whatever the Latin inscribed on the city's coat of arms, the true motto of the Parisian is, as Pierre Daninos pointed out in *Les Carnets du Major Thompson*: "*On se défend*," which might be translated as "Keep your guard up".

Many foreigners—and especially Americans—never manage to understand, let alone appreciate, the Parisian attitude. For some strange reason

An Iron Giant Rises

While it was under construction the 984-foot-high tower designed by Gustave Eiffel for the 1889 Paris Universal Exposition inevitably attracted sightseers and artists, who recorded its progress with engravings such as these. For two years workmen laboured to erect the colossus, planting masonry piers 40 feet into the earth and joining 12,000 iron girders with two and a half million rivets. It was the world's tallest structure until 1930 when New York's 1,048-foot Chrysler Building superseded it.

Exposition visitors clamber to the top in 1889.

Sightseers inspect one of the tower's half-finished foundations of big stone blocks.

The completed tower proudly flies the French tricolour high above the city.

The unfinished hulk of the structure looms above men building exhibition halls.

that I have never really fathomed, most Americans expect other people to be "nice". Parisians aren't "nice". They are cantankerous and irritable, like spoiled brats. But behind this apparent childishness there lurks within the Parisian a very adult, world-weary, self-mocking smile—an unsuspected and usually undetected modesty—that represents a kind of wisdom most other people rarely attain. For visitors who cannot perceive this self-mockery behind the aggressiveness, life in Paris can be a real trial; they don't get the joke. Parisians are just as irritable and aggressive with one another as they are with foreigners, but this does not soothe the wound. I have known dozens of Americans who have left this fantastic city feeling disappointed, hurt and unloved. They never made their peace with Paris because they could never bring themselves around to thinking like a Frenchman. Admittedly, that's a difficult jump to make, but the reward of truly understanding Paris is worth it a thousand times over—even if it means swallowing a few affronts along the way.

Take the case of *Mauvais Caractère*. He is one of our neighbourhood fixtures: a baker who owns a little shop on the corner of Rue du Four and Rue des Canettes. I have no idea of his real name, because for years my wife and I have called him simply *Mauvais Caractère*—Sourpuss. For longer than I care to remember, we had been swearing to start boycotting him in retaliation for his permanent grumpiness and the impolite grunts with which he infallibly answered all our questions. *Mauvais Caractère* was a real bastard. We'd get even with him some day. Only there was one big problem: without question, he baked the best bread and tarts in the area. A *baguette* loaf from *Mauvais Caractère* made the other bakers of the Sixth Arrondissement seem like cardboard dealers. Stubbornly, in his ill-humoured way, he continued to bake bread in the old fashion of the artisans, refusing the chemical whiteners and additives that have now infiltrated, alas, even Paris. Always he gave his customers full value, with foods as delicious as they were pure.

Old Sourpuss presided over his dark little shop like a tyrant, forever wearing the same red sweater, his greying hair combed severely back, a Gauloise on his lip and a disdainful challenge in his eye. Even in his manner of arranging his wares he seemed to be defying the world. The *pâtisserie* that he put on display every morning seemed shrivelled, colour-less and sloppy compared with the bright perfections shown in other shops. Yet *his* had the best flavour and truest ingredients.

One day, when I went by to pick up a *baguette*, I had an inspiration. As I crossed the sill of his shop I threw out a breezy greeting: "*Bonjour, patron.* Still mad at the world?"

He hesitated in the briefest of double-takes, then broke into a huge smile. "It's the only way," he confided. "Between you and me" (and he leaned over the counter like a conspirator) "the only reason I keep on working is to torment the others."

This boulangerie-pâtisserie (bakery and pastry shop), which happens to share part of its premises with a flower seller, still retains a turn-of-the-century charm. Boulangeries, found in almost every street in the city, offer Parisians fresh-baked bread every day.

Mauvais Caractère and I are good friends now. And I must confess that when I'm in his shop I enjoy watching cantankerous native-born Parisians shrink under his glower. But even now—years after that day when I finally broke through his defences—he is still too pridefully modest to admit that he bakes good bread for any reason but to torment the others.

Sourpuss the Baker will always remain my personal metaphor for the Parisian personality. But there are two other stories that sum it up for me just as accurately, and from different angles. The first story I heard from a young lady of German parentage who had spent most of her childhood in France and therefore knew both countries well and spoke both languages fluently. One summer she and her husband, also German, signed up for a sailing course at a seamanship and navigation school on a rocky island off the Britanny coast. The school was notorious for its toughness—all business and military-style control. Boys and girls slept separately, even married couples; quarters were spartan, showers cold, meals frugal, discipline tight. But at her course, she told me, the discipline lasted no more than 48 hours under the ministration of her Parisian fellow students. Once the novelty of taking orders had worn off (it was seriously damaged after the first day), the Parisians reverted to their true nature.

The sailboats were anchored about a hundred yards offshore and every morning the same unavoidable, anarchic dialogue repeated itself: "Who's going to carry the equipment bag? Who's going to fetch the oars?"

After a long, stubborn silence, the eyes began shifting back and forth, the shoulders shrugging, the veiled accusations and justifications flying.

"I got the oars yesterday."

"You did not. You were hiding in the latrine."

"Well, I was sick."

"It's not my job. My turn doesn't come until the day after tomorrow."

And so it continued with many sighs and gestures until my friend, the German-born lady, went away unbidden and got the oars *and* the equipment bag. The men were not in the least shamed or discomfited to see a woman doing their work. In fact, they admired her efficiency, told her so, and encouraged her to become the permanent bag-carrier. When it was time to push the big, broad-beamed rowing boat into the water, and then to row it, the same chaotic disagreement broke out as energetically as before. The air rang with cries of anguish, quickly turning to satisfied raillery when the German couple took the oars and rowed the parliament of Parisians out to their yachts.

"*Ah, là-là,*" said my friend. "What a vacation! If it had been only Germans on that island, we would have marched the rowing boat down the beach in lockstep. But I think I like better the French style."

My second tale may be apocryphal, but it sounds as though it *should* have happened. The time was the early 1950s. President Vincent Auriol was showing some now-forgotten visitor around his official residence, the Élysée Palace. He made a special point of leading his guest to the presidential bathroom, where wash-basin, tub and bidet stood like elegant, gold-fixtured monuments to the turn of the century. "*Et le plus drôle,*" said Auriol, raising an index finger for emphasis, "*c'est que ça marche*"— "The funniest thing of all is that they work." Perhaps Charles de Gaulle, with his great dignity, lofty intelligence—and his pomposity, too—represented La France. But for me it is Vincent Auriol who represents Paris.

Not without chagrin, I left Paris at the end of my fellowship, wondering all the while how long it would be before I could return. I knew I would be back, but the "when" was very uncertain. As it happened, my luck could scarcely have been better. That very autumn I became a reporter for LIFE Magazine; within six months I was back in Paris as a European correspondent—on a real salary, with an apartment of my own. My poor student days were now far behind me. I even managed to reconcile myself, for better or worse, to the Right Bank. But I never did quite lose the student mentality, the pleasure in discovering an off-beat section of town I had not seen before—a new bistro, a new phrase in the vulgar Parisian *argot*, slang. I cannot say that since then I have developed all the multiple virtues of the true Parisian, but I do think I now share something of the same temperament. For me there is no possible other way. Paris and its attitude towards the 60 or 70 or 80 years we are given on this planet have gradually become imperatives for me. Paris is my home, my teacher.

I love Paris. Not, I hope, with the sappy sentimentality of that lyricist who rhymed "drizzles" and "sizzles" (beware of sentimentality), but as

On the Champs-Élysées, an elderly Parisian sits at a sidewalk

one who gets up with the city every morning and sees it without make-up, through illusionless eyes. Paris has plenty of faults and blemishes, but it is still one of the last cities on the face of this earth where one can live gracefully, intelligently and happily. It is a place to work, certainly—France is probably the most centralized country in the world, and Paris is the centre —but it also is, *par excellence*, a place to live. No one flees Paris for the suburbs except those who can't afford to stay; it is still a privilege to dwell "in town". Of course, the city is expensive; volumes of sociological studies could be written about the economic injustice that drives the poorer folk into the peripheral bedroom boroughs. But what is most striking about Paris, what sets it apart from so many other great cities, is the fact that its central core is as lively and attractive and desirable as ever.

What makes it so livable? Again, I have to come back to the concept of humanity. You can feel at ease with your soul and your surroundings in Paris. You have the very pertinent certitude that this city and its inhabitants have their priorities in the right order. It is a city made for human beings, just as New York is a city made for power and money, and modern Moscow has turned into one made for . . . trucks.

The scale is human. Although Paris is vast, sprawling and heavily populated (more than 8,000,000 people, counting the suburbs), it is never overpowering or impersonal. With some modern exceptions, it is a city of buildings six, seven and eight storeys high, almost all of them made with blocks of the warm, cream-coloured limestone that underlies the Parisian Basin (the city stands precariously over the honeycomb of its own ancient quarries), and decorated with the black wrought iron whose working is a minor French art. The stone and iron give a consistent character and architectural theme, but within that homogeneity is a most tremendous variety of style and inspiration.

The roofs alone make a fascinating study. The only drawback to roof-gazing is the irritating tendency to march upon a dog's *besoin* (dogs are not curbed in Paris), but even that hazard has its sunny side: according to French folklore it is a guarantee of good luck that will follow soon. Mind you, that applies only when stepped on with the left foot; the right foot, apparently, offers no compensations.

Although they may appear to blanket all the city, the buildings of Paris often conceal behind their façades that marvellous medieval vestige, the inner courtyard. The faces of the buildings may be blank stone, but once you push the buzzer at one of those formidable, green front doors, another world appears as the doors swing open—complete with flowers and trees and lawns. There are thousands of secret gardens to be discovered in Paris at the push of a buzzer.

The variety of courtyards is more than matched by the unpredictable jumble of streets. Some streets are descended from Roman *vias*, some from footpaths of the Middle Ages, while others—most of the straight and wide ones—date from the 19th Century, when city planners first began to make an impact. Many have names that are reminders of a time beyond living memory when they served purposes other than crossing points for automobiles: Rue des Mauvais-Garçons (Bad Boys' Street), Rue de la Grande-Truanderie (Great Knavery Street—opposite, incidentally, Little Knavery Street), Rue du Chat-qui-Pêche (Fishing Cat Street), Rue des Quatre Vents (Street of the Four Winds), Rue du Four (Oven Street), and Rue Montorgueil (Prideful Mountain Street—an example of early Parisian humour, since the mountain in question was a medieval garbage heap). Why do Americans name their streets with such triteness: Maple, Oak, Walnut, First, Second, Third. Because we had no Middle Ages?

The streets of Paris are safe. Even long after dark, muggings and molestings and purse-snatchings are rarities. I need have no anxiety when my wife and child go out after nightfall, and I don't want to live in any city where I do. An American friend of mine lives in the heart of the Pigalle prostitution district, and whenever he passes the ladies of the streets, some of them grizzled veterans who have been walking their beat for 20 years or more, they greet him with a polite *bonjour* or *bonsoir*, often taking the time to inquire about his children back in the States. The French are a civil people, as well as a civilized one.

Paris is always surprising and enjoyable, even in the backward little districts that the casual tourist rarely sees. It ranks far behind many great cities in terms of parks but it is full of trees which in spring and summer turn the streets into long parallactic tunnels running down to another *arrondissement*, another village. Les Gobelins in the south is as different from La Goutte d'Or in the north as Auteuil in the west is different from Charonne in the east. All of these villages had their own distinct personalities in days when the city of Paris was limited to the Île de la Cité, the Latin Quarter and the Marais. The city grew and absorbed them, but they still maintain an independent flavour of their own. Within the villages are quarters and sometimes, within the quarters, *îlots*—islets, each with its own character. Paris is all variety, change, surprise and beauty.

There are a thousand places of beauty, and even the most commonplace still give a catch in the throat when I see them. I never tire of the view from the Pont des Arts at night—of the Seine branching right and left from the tip of the Île de la Cité, where the weeping willow, known as *le Vert-Galant* (in honour of Henri IV, the most Parisian of French kings) arcs its limbs over the cobbled walkway and into the water.

The French have a genius for the well-made gesture, for presentation, whether it be a raw *faux filet* (sirloin) on a bed of parsley in a butcher's window, or a dapper policeman, peaked cap angled low over one eye, jauntily directing traffic with his white gloves and stick, or the cut of an Yves St-Laurent gown and the ambiguous smile of the *Parisienne* within it. Or, for that matter, the little old lady I saw last spring at a sidewalk café on

Place Edmond-Rostand, opposite the Luxembourg Gardens. She was seated alone, immaculately dressed and looking as elegant and fragile as a dried flower. Before her, on one of the small, round marble tables, was a crystal glass and a half-bottle of champagne in an ice bucket. What was her private celebration? Whatever it was, she was doing it right.

Paris is very much a feminine city, in the most flattering sense of that word. The women of Paris are its strength and its joy; they are at ease with themselves, their condition and their men, to a degree that non-French women rarely achieve. If, for millions of filmgoers throughout the world, Catherine Deneuve symbolizes perfect, luxurious beauty, how many of them know that she is also thoughtful and astute? She is typically Parisian.

(A thought occurs to me: most Americans I have known who hated Paris and left it with disappointment in their hearts have been women. Could there be an undeclared and undefined hostility between women and Paris? A rivalry? A jealousy?)

Essentially, too, Paris is a city that concerns itself with life and living, right here and now, and—as was impressed upon me in lesson one on board *Flandre*—that inevitably involves treating food and its eating with the greatest respect. Later I shall be describing some of the finest, most elegant restaurants in Paris (and consequently some of the best in the world), but I myself will always treasure the memory of more modest establishments, the ones that really prove how profound is the city's love and regard for a proper meal properly eaten.

Every day I buy my newspapers from a lady on the corner of Rue de Rennes and Rue du Vieux Colombier. One rainy winter's afternoon, around two o'clock, I walked up to the blue, plywood shelter where she holds court in her ragged parka, enthroned among stacks of papers and magazines, and as I absently reached into my pocket for change I became aware of the most extraordinary odours wafting upwards from *France-Soir*, *le Monde* and *le Figaro*. Then I heard the scraping of fork and knife against plate, saw the glass of red wine on the counter beside her. Here was no vulgar sandwich; lunch was far too serious a thing to be abandoned to mere frivolities. Madame was having *blanquette de veau*.

"*Bon appétit, Madame*," I said, handing over my francs.

"*Merci, Monsieur*," she replied, carefully placing fork and knife at the edge of her plate before giving me my paper. "*Et bonne journée.*" That is food, and that is Paris.

A City of Eloquent Faces

As varied as a group of minor characters from a novel by Balzac, war veterans wait in the shadow of the Arc de Triomphe during a Remembrance Day service.

The faces of Parisians seem shaped as much by character as by Gallic inheritance. The portrait gallery on these and the following pages offers glimpses of some of those faces in the moments that occur when a person feels unquestionably at home, in touch with his feelings, unmindful of the stranger's eye upon him. What shines through each visage is an intensity of emotion. And each projects that characteristic self-confidence that foreigners at times interpret as arrogance or, when Parisians are animated into witty volubility (as they often are), as cynical frivolity. It is probably nearer the truth, however, to say that such assuredness is a reflection of wisdom based on experience acquired during the 2,000 years of the city's existence. For in their maturity, Parisians know there are no real surprises to come; they have seen them all.

By his ancient hoist, a wine merchant gives a look that is neither friendly nor hostile, but probing.

At a rare moment when no clients are in his bar, the owner (left) muses in seemingly gloomy silence, while mother and baby quietly ponder their own thoughts.

Smiling suavely from beneath his jaunty cap, a fishmonger savours life from his stall in a Montmartre market.

A Parisian brings severely critical concentration to bear on the tactical problems of his game of boules, one among many in progress in the Bois de Boulogne.

At Longchamps racetrack, a favourite gathering place for "Le Tout Paris" (the city's fashionable set), an elegant woman effortlessly projects Parisian chic.

/31

Immaculate attire bolstering natural self-possession, a contemplative man smooths his moustache.

At ease in the Luxembourg Gardens, a bourgeois abandons himself to sombre reflection.

Even when whiling away a day at cards, an elderly Parisienne maintains the mien that characterizes her city: self-confidence with just a touch of superiority.

2

The Gothic Core

Before there was France—even before there were a people called the French—there was Paris. It all began on an island in the middle of a broad, powerfully flowing and fish-rich river: the Seine. Here a group of Celtic tribesmen known as the Parisii settled, and you will be pleased to know that they were ferocious right from the start—*mauvais caractères* in fact. They fortified their village with earthen breastworks reinforced by tree trunks. It was called "Lutèce", possibly meaning "between the waters". Over the years they filled in shoals and joined near-by gravel banks until they had a solid and safe chunk of land. Today that original island home bears one of the magic names of Western civilization: Île de la Cité.

If ever a traveller were unfortunate enough to be limited to just one hour in Paris, he would do well to spend it on the Île de la Cité. The island is the bull's-eye, the symbolic centre, of this most centralized of all countries. All distances are measured from Kilomètre Zéro: a brass, compass-like star embedded in the pavement outside the West door of the Cathedral of Notre-Dame, the Île's most prominent landmark. More than any other part of Paris, this island spells history and tradition. Here the Roman legions of Julius Caesar established a permanent garrison half a century before the birth of Christ; and here, for centuries, the succeeding French kings installed themselves in the great stone palace, parts of which still stand near the western tip of the island.

No one has ever accused the Parisians of being slow when it comes to business. The Parisii were mostly fishermen and boatmen, but it didn't take them long to discover commerce—that great, primal motor of city building. Lutèce lay at a natural ford along one of antiquity's most important commercial pathways. To the north were the British Isles, where primitive mines yielded ores rich in tin and lead; to the south was Rome, almost as avid for metals as it was for power. And here, between them, were the Parisii, who connected their island to either shore—the Right Bank to the north, the Left Bank to the south—with two spindly bridges. More than likely they extracted tolls from those early traders who wanted to get across the Seine with dry feet; Parisians have rarely made a habit of giving things away. In addition, there was good soil for producing oats, wheat and barley, plenty of fish to be caught in the Seine's pure waters, and plenty of freight to be carried up and downstream. Lutèce prospered.

Whenever there was prosperity in view, or a town as strategically located as Lutèce, the Romans could be counted on to react with their unfailing opportunism: I-want-it-and-here-I-come. They came in 53 B.C., led by

Bathed in light tinted by the oldest stained glass windows in Paris, a group of nuns visit La Sainte-Chapelle on Île de la Cité. When the chapel was built for King Louis IX in the 13th Century, its great expanse of windows stunned Parisians, who had never before seen a structure virtually without walls, its roof supported only by slim pillars and buttresses.

Julius Caesar, who was on the march to bring rebel Gallic tribes to heel. The Senones and the Carnutes, tribes from the districts of Sens and Orléans, had refused to send delegates to an Assembly of Gauls convened by the Romans at Amiens. Caesar, marching directly south from the Amienois, made camp on the boat-shaped island in the Seine. The position so impressed him that he promptly decided that "Lutetia of the Parisii", as he called it in his *Gallic Wars*, should be the new meeting place of the Gallic chiefs. The following year, when the Roman Emperor-to-be had departed leaving behind occupying troops, the Parisii joined a general uprising and fought ferociously on the site where today the Eiffel Tower stands, before being finally routed by Roman legionnaires led by Titus Labienus. Then, true to character, the Parisii burned their town to the ground rather than hand it over to the victor.

Labienus was the first in a long line of "Little Caesars" who demanded passive obedience of these people but discovered instead the intransigent reef of the *mauvais caractère parisien*. The Parisii eventually adapted themselves to their Roman rulers, as they would to their own native-born princes once the Romans left. But in Paris the relationship between leader and people has always remained tumultuous, the public order precarious. The citizens have never submitted easily to severe discipline or to the kind of crippling taxation imposed by the Romans and subsequent rulers. Over the next two thousand years the city was to see more than a dozen major, bloody uprisings.

Of all the alien autocrats of Paris only one created a truly favourable impression: Flavius Claudius Julian Caesar, nephew of Constantine the Great, who made the city his administrative headquarters in A.D. 358. This young man, then in his mid-twenties, found the one sure way to make friends of the native populace: he cut taxation by two-thirds.

Lutèce was a booming garrison town by now, spreading out across the river to the hill known today as the Montagne-Ste-Geneviève. There the Romans built themselves a luxurious, white-stoned city, complete with all the usual accoutrements: aqueduct, baths, forum, a theatre (in the vicinity of the present-day Rue Racine) and an arena (near the Rue Monge) where gladiator games were held. Even then Paris was a good assignment. "I was in winter quarters at my dear Lutetia," wrote the future emperor Julian, "for thus is the town of the Parisii called in Gaul. It is on a small island with wooden bridges giving access to the two shores. The river rarely swells or diminishes; as it is in summer, so it remains in winter. It is a pleasure to drink the water, for it is very pure and agreeable."

Briefly, under Julian, Paris had its first taste of being a capital city, and as long as he had his government there it was virtually the seat of the Roman Empire in the west. Unfortunately, Julian was able to remain in Paris for only three winters, between campaigns. And he and his countrymen were so certain of the invincibility of their empire that they departed

High above Paris, Notre-Dame's most famous grotesque stands at his lonely post, defending the cathedral with his fearsome appearance. All of the original medieval gargoyles were removed in the 18th Century when some, weakened by 600 years of weathering, began crashing to the pavement 200 feet below. This figure is a 19th-Century replacement.

without troubling to build defensive walls around their *oppidum* (town). They paid dearly for the error when the barbarian invaders came from the north in malignant waves and drove the Romans from the region. Left to fend for themselves again, the Parisii withdrew to their island, their *cité*, this time fortifying it with building stones from the Romans' abandoned settlement on the Left Bank. And with independence temporarily restored, the island took on the name of its original inhabitants, the name that would identify it forever with their tribe. Lutèce became Paris.

In A.D. 508, Clovis, king of the Salian Franks, master of the ancient imperial province of Belgica Secunda (the northern half of present-day France), left Rheims to make Paris his capital, to rule from the palace of the Roman governors on the Île de la Cité. Christianity was now taking firm hold. Clovis and his successors in Paris began wresting a single nation out of the patchwork of duchies that lay all around them. And as the French nation began creating a uniquely French civilization, so Paris, the island stronghold, once again grew steadily outwards, far across both banks of the Seine, eventually to become the greatest city in the Western world.

The ancient palace of the Romans remained the home of French kings until, in the mid-14th Century, a citizens revolt made "downtown" life too risky and they moved over to the Right Bank, to a citadel that was both modern and easier to defend: the Louvre. But occasionally, when the French nation wished to make a symbol of an incarceration, one part of the old palace continued to retain its original function. This was the infamous prison known as the Conciergerie. Various regicides and would-be regicides were locked up in its stony keep; so were Madame Du Barry, mistress of Louis XV, and—most famous of all—the wife of Louis XVI, the witless Marie-Antoinette, who ingenuously suggested that the poor eat cake since they no longer had any bread. The Conciergerie became the ante-chamber of the guillotine.

The palace is peaceful and bureaucratic now; it is the site of the courts of the Palais de Justice, with the police headquarters and chamber of commerce across the street. The Conciergerie continues to be partly used for prisoners awaiting trial. But the palace's former glory is most evident in La Sainte-Chapelle, the stunningly beautiful stone-and-glass reliquary that Louis IX ordered to be built in the mid-13th Century as a spectacular gesture of piety. It is one of two masterpieces of Gothic architecture on the island—the other being, of course, Notre-Dame. Every time I visit La Sainte-Chapelle, climb up that dank spiral stone stairway in the dark, and then step into the brilliance of that huge, delicate vault lit from all sides by the oldest and most sublime stained glass in Paris, I am as dazzled by the colour as I am by the knowledge that it is over 700 years old.

The monarch responsible for this glorious chapel was certainly a great man (he was eventually canonized as Saint Louis), but he does not strike me as being particularly representative of the Parisian spirit. Firstly, he was indefatigably pious and insufferably proselytical—a king who would wash the feet of blind beggars and who was forever going off on crusades, ultimately dying on his travels to convert the Sultan of Tunisia. Secondly, he was interminably gullible—paying out fabulous sums of money for such improbable "holy relics" as a fragment of the spear that stabbed Christ, a sample of the Virgin Mary's milk, of Jesus' swaddling clothes. Never mind— what counted was that he put up the cash, and hired the architects and artists and stonemasons to build the most beautiful jewel-box the world has ever seen: a shrine for his two most treasured purchases—the Crown of Thorns and two pieces of the True Cross.

To find a king far more representative of the spirit of Paris one need go only a short way beyond Louis' Sainte-Chapelle to the western tip of the Île de la Cité, where the Seine flows away towards the Pont des Arts, the Pont du Carrousel, past the Eiffel Tower and finally to the sea at Le Havre. Here is the Square du Vert-Galant, a tree-shaded garden much favoured by lovers, painters, sightseers, guitar-players, beggars, poets and students —by all the characteristic fauna that makes the street life of the old sections of Paris so sympathetic. There, beneath the drooping arms of the willow tree that takes the name of the square, looms the equestrian figure of that incurable romantic, Henri IV. Brave, boisterous, compassionate and sensual, the good King Henri was called *le Vert-Galant* in the 16th Century because of his unquenchable fondness for the ladies (*Vert-Galant* might be freely translated as "lively ladies' man" or, more vulgarly, "skirt-chaser"). The well-watered willow, whose leaves always turn green before any other tree in Paris, is a fitting symbol for the man who had at least three "official" mistresses when he was king and an untold number of *conquêtes galantes*. Need I add that Henri was the most popular of all French kings?

Henri IV was a sceptical Protestant and leader of the Huguenots, but he didn't hesitate to abjure his religion and convert to Catholicism in Notre-Dame with the immortal words: "Paris is well worth a mass." About the only thing for which his subjects reproached him was the excessive spending of his first wife on all manner of Parisian fripperies. Marguerite de Valois was her name; an admirably complex woman, as talented as she was cultivated. She wrote poetry, spoke brilliantly, and was resolutely modern in thought and manner. Unfortunately, she was also, as one French scholar put it, "*victime de sa nymphomanie*", and finally became impossible as a consort, even for *le Vert-Galant*.

A story from that period tells of King Henri boarding a ferry to cross the Seine. The boatman, who had his back turned to his sovereign, was heard to mumble a long complaint that could not be more Parisian: "We're paying more taxes than during the war. The King's a good enough fellow, but he's got a wicked strumpet on his hands who's driving us all to ruin

This immense Gothic hall, embedded among the buildings of the Palais de Justice, survives from the 13th-Century palace of Louis IX. The hall is part of the Conciergerie, originally the residence of the master of the king's household but used as a prison since 1392. During the Terror of 1793-94 more than 2,000 prisoners passed through it on their way to the guillotine.

with the pretty dresses and baubles he gives her every day, and it's us poor honest folk who suffer and pay for it all."

Henri finally had the marriage annulled but, unlike Henry VIII of England, he didn't feel compelled to have his cast-off wife executed. He exiled her instead. He then married the stodgy, predictable Marie de' Medici, sired four children and eventually allowed Marguerite to return to Paris, where she ended her days painted and corseted, chasing young men and writing her memoirs. Henri's last, brotherly advice to her was: "Stop taking the night for day and the day for night."

Le Vert-Galant was the first king to recognize that the true strength and power of this aristocratic city lay with the bourgeoisie and to act on that realization by officially associating them with his vision of urbanization. He pointed the way to great civic development schemes, and he was the visionary behind two of the most gracious features of Paris today: Place des Vosges on the Right Bank and Place Dauphine on the Île de la Cité.

The arcaded Place des Vosges—originally called Place Royale—sprang from Henri's idea of cleaning up an insalubrious, rundown area around a horse market near the Bastille and constructing a residential square. He laid down the model, then called in bourgeois promoters and builders to have it erected in geometrically perfect style. Completed in 1612, the *place* immediately became the most elegant and sought-after address in Paris, attracting Cardinal Richelieu himself.

Two years after that construction began, Henri ceded to a developer some land near the bottom tip of Île de la Cité. Previously it had been a royal orchard and occasional execution ground; now it was transformed

Below Notre-Dame's spire, both the eastern end of the Île de la Cité and, beyond a narrow arm of the Seine, the Île St-Louis bask in cloud-piercing sunshine.

into Place Dauphine, a triangular block of dwellings around tournament grounds suitable for plays, jousting and equestrian ballets. Today not much survives of Henri's original Place Dauphine; the entire block of buildings that formed the base of the triangle was pulled down a century ago (a pompous stairway of the Palais de Justice occupies its place). But even with the changes wrought by generations and generations of landlords and developers, Place Dauphine remains the loveliest residential area on an island otherwise devoted to administration.

Senselessly, Henri was assassinated before he could realize all his exciting plans for improving the city—stabbed to death by the religious fanatic, François Ravaillac. France's most popular king died in the Louvre, and never was vengeance so fiercely demanded and met. Ravaillac was dragged barefoot through the streets, from the Conciergerie to Notre-Dame, where he was forced to kneel and pray, then carted to the Place de Grève where, two centuries later, the guillotine was to make its grim début. For Ravaillac the blade of the guillotine would have been a welcome mercy. Instead, he lived to see his right hand burned off (the one that held the dagger), to have holes carved in his chest and limbs, and then to have the cavities filled with boiling oil and melted lead. Finally he was drawn and quartered, his remains thrown to dogs running wild in the street.

Henri IV was so greatly loved that 179 years later, in 1789, as the Revolution erupted, citizens compelled aristocrats passing by to leave their carriages and kneel before the statue of "the people's king". Three years later, when a revolutionary edict decreed the destruction of all royal statues, le Vert-Galant on his pedestal in the bow of Île de la Cité was the last to go, and then only after his loyal admirers had delayed the demolition squads by blocking the Pont Neuf. The present statue, erected in 1818, was made of bronze from statues destroyed by the revolutionaries. Today it is still gaily saluted by Parisians who have never forgotten the joyous king who loved life and women, and who dreamed of the day when every man in Paris would have "a chicken in the pot for Sunday dinner".

At the other end of the Île de la Cité, on an otherwise undistinguished wall facing out over the Quai aux Fleurs, there is a faded yellowish plaque that, with the statue of le Vert-Galant, is one of my favourite reminders of passion in Paris. It reads: "*Ancienne habitation d'Héloïse et d'Abélard, 1118, rebâtie en 1849*", and it records the residence there of a pair of immortal lovers who equal Tristram and Isolde or Romeo and Juliet as supreme symbols of earthly passion, but who, unlike those figures of fiction, truly existed and truly suffered. There was nothing spiritual about their love: it was searing, sexual. That, too, is Paris.

Pierre Abélard, a Breton from the neighbourhood of Nantes, was 27 years old when he arrived in Paris at the dawn of the 12th Century. Already a brilliant and precocious scholar, he was to become France's most famous and controversial teacher, the first great rebel intellectual to pit cold logic against theological dogma and to challenge the pervasive ecclesiastical establishment. He built up a following of thousands of young students and, by teaching on the Left Bank outside the confines of the cloister of Notre-Dame, he was one of the founding spirits of the Latin Quarter and what would become the University of Paris. The name of Abélard stands for learning, perhaps the greatest of Paris' glories. Yet today he is remembered firstly as a tragic lover and only secondly as a professor who espoused relentless, dialectic and independent thought.

Abélard was 35, already a renowned teacher, when he was invited into the home of Canon Fulbert of Paris to instruct his 18-year-old niece Héloïse. Soon tutor and pupil became lovers. "Under the pretext of studying, we gave ourselves over to love," Abélard wrote much later. "The books were opened, but more words of love were spoken than words of philosophy, and kisses were more numerous than explanations. My hands came more often to her breast than to our books; love was reflected in our eyes more often than reading directed them towards the texts."

Héloïse bore him a son (discreetly delivered at his sister's home in Brittany) and later they married secretly. It was intended to be a well-kept secret so that no scandal might prejudice Abélard's career as a teacher and a cleric in minor orders. But the disapproving uncle talked, and to protect her husband Héloïse publicly denied her marriage and entered a convent. Canon Fulbert immediately leapt to the conclusion that Abélard was abandoning his young niece, and the act of vengeance that this wretch paid local thugs to perform could not have been less Christian.

Abélard himself described the moment in his aptly-named *Historia Calamitatum* ("History of My Troubles"): "One night, when I was asleep in my room, my servant, who had been bribed, unlocked my door to bandits led by Fulbert who, throwing themselves upon me, made me undergo the most barbarous and shameful of vengeances, a vengeance so infamous that everyone heard the news with stupefaction: steel separated from me the parts of my body by which I had committed the sins for which they reproached me."

Such was the impact of that atrocity that *abélardiser* came into popular parlance as a new verb, meaning "to castrate". The two thugs directly reponsible had their eyes put out and, under the legal precept of *talion* (an eye for an eye), the authorities had them deprived of their manhood. Fulbert lost his position as Canon of Notre-Dame and had his possessions confiscated. And the two lovers? Héloïse remained in the nunnery and eventually became mother superior of a convent founded by her husband. Abélard became a monk and a hermit, but later returned to Paris where, in spite of his condition, he taught as fiercely as ever on the Montagne-Ste-Geneviève. When he died his body was secretly removed to Héloïse's convent and, 22 years later, on her death, they were reunited. Today they

Seen through a black tracery of leafless trees, the massive west front of Notre-Dame glows in the russet warmth of floodlights on a winter night. The great rose window, 31 feet in diameter, combines delicacy with strength in a miracle of medieval art and architecture.

lie side by side in the Paris cemetery, Père Lachaise, where their tomb is an object of pilgrimage still.

I know of no other city in the world where love is so openly, even proudly expressed as in Paris. From "*les amoureux qui s'bécot'ent sur les bancs publics* (the lovers who kiss on park benches)" to the couples enlaced on the grass of Bois de Boulogne; to the short-stay *hôtels de passe* where lustful couples may order three-course meals and/or champagne, the descendants of Héloïse and Abélard enjoy Paris, as they enjoy each other, to a degree that always surprises the first-time visitor to the city. Everywhere, it seems, couples are kissing, often with such abandon that the casual observer feels constrained to turn his eyes away, out of a respect for a privacy to which the lovers are obviously indifferent.

Since in my first chapter I chose a president of the Republic to exemplify the Parisian mentality, let me pick another one as the paragon of Parisian sensuality—His Excellency Félix Faure, one of the several chiefs of state of the Third Republic. President Faure managed to end his mandate and his own life in 1899 by expiring in the Élysée Palace in the arms of his mistress. The manner of his death caused a scandal among the bluestockings lurking around the periphery of Parisian life. But it made him a hero—far more than his political achievements could ever have done—to the vast majority of Parisians.

In days when it has become fashionable, at least in some Anglo-Saxon countries, to exacerbate the battle of the sexes into a sullen stand-off, it is reassuring to know that in Paris—the city that knows how to live— enthusiasm for natural physical contact still reigns.

In 1163, one year before Héloïse and Abélard were reunited in death, Pope Alexander III laid the foundation stone of the most extraordinary building that Paris, or indeed France, had ever seen: a monstrous edifice that would take more than a century to complete: the Cathedral of Notre-Dame. A house of God it most assuredly was, but Notre-Dame de Paris stood for temporal ambition as well. It was a political gesture, just as much as a testimonial of faith. If Notre-Dame is awesome today, think of the effect it had in those medieval times—the city was only a bishopric then, under the authority of the archbishop of Sens. By building a cathedral (142 yards long, 312 feet high) that was out of all proportion to the size and importance of Paris, the kings who watched it rising over a 182-year period were affirming to their countrymen, and to the world beyond, that whatever the pretensions of Aquitaine, Burgundy or Brittany, it was the duke of the Île de France who would be supreme. Faith alone was not enough to bring the nation together. It required faith and power; and superb architecture represents both forces all over Paris.

What can one say about this most famous of all cathedrals that has not already been written? More than the Eiffel Tower, more than zee French

With wordless movement a mime acts out a story in Place du Parvis, a square in front of Notre-Dame frequented by street entertainers. Mime has flourished in Paris since medieval times, but became particularly attractive to young performers after Frenchman Marcel Marceau won recognition in the 1950s as the world's greatest exponent of the art.

can-can, as much as the island on which it stands, Notre-Dame—Our Lady—is the symbol of Paris. It was the city's first great affirmation of primacy and throughout history it has remained its heart, its focus. There, Henri IV foreswore his Protestantism. There, Henry VI of England, aged ten, was crowned King of France. There, a little Corsican megalomaniac named Bonaparte grabbed the crown from the Pope's hands and crowned himself Emperor. There, when the firebrands of the French Revolution wished to seal forever their break with the past, they underlined their point by converting the cathedral into a Temple of Reason, enthroning opera dancer Mademoiselle Maillard on the high altar as Goddess of Reason and setting up statues of Voltaire and Rousseau in place of those of the saints. There, in May, 1940, the French government gathered for a high mass as priests called upon Saint-Louis and Joan of Arc to deliver their country from the Nazi panzers. Four years later Notre-Dame was the scene of a mass of thanksgiving as the Allies liberated Paris.

Although Gothic architecture, as typified by Notre-Dame, was invented in Paris, one should remember that the results were not always viewed with the awed, whispery respect that now suffuses the cathedral. For instance, in the Middle Ages, the statuary crowding the three main portals of Notre-Dame was painted in garish polychrome and the common folk (who had neither books nor radio nor television) "read" the sculptures as one would a comic book, delighting in the allegorical scenes—some of them saintly, some funny, and some even pornographic. (Some of the ironwork was thought to have been fashioned by Satan himself.)

Over the centuries tens of thousands of Sunday painters have reverently reproduced in painstaking detail Notre-Dame's twin towers and flying buttresses, but how many would dare treat Our Lady with the impiety she inspired in some of France's greatest writers? For Rabelais and Victor Hugo, she brought out the grotesque. What was Quasimodo, the hunchback of Notre-Dame, but an earlier—and much more interesting—version of King Kong? And Rabelais' giant, Gargantua, captured the Parisian spirit when he climbed the towers of Notre-Dame to urinate abundantly upon the common folk below him—and stole the cathedral's bells for good measure. How vulgar. How funny. How Parisian.

Much of that medieval lustiness remains today, in spite of all the moralizers, prigs and salvationists who would have Notre-Dame be nothing more than a repository for prayers. The Place du Parvis, the pretty, grassy mall stretching in front of the cathedral, is, like the Square du Vert-Galant, a favourite gathering place for hippies, lovers and unemployables. Occasionally, the police—*flics*, as they are called—round up the idlers or shoo them away, but their heart isn't in it. The fauna returns, and I am thankful for it; the mall would be a bore without them—like George Bernard Shaw's vision of an icy, pure and utterly tiresome Heaven. Not so long ago—in 1971 to be exact—a daring young man named Philippe

Petit amused the Parisians and earned himself instant fame by stretching a tightrope between the towers of Notre-Dame and strolling across before a *flic* or a deacon could stop him. Our Lady of Paris was his springboard to fortune. Petit followed up his triumph by performing the same stunt between the 110-storey towers of the New York Trade Center, and it landed him a fat contract with an American circus.

North of Notre-Dame, tucked away between the Tribunal de Commerce and the old hospital known as Hôtel-Dieu, is another of the reasons why I like the Île de la Cité: the Marché aux Fleurs. Inaugurated by a decree of Napoleon in 1809, the Flower Market is still an oasis of 19th-Century leisureliness and ease in the very heart of the city. The cast-iron and glass sheds that shelter the merchants are anachronistic, to be sure; but it is the great wisdom of Paris not to fear anachronism. So far, the market has successfully resisted all the encroachments of so-called progress and avoided the modern real-estate promoters who have sacked and pillaged other, less protected quarters of the city. The plants and potted trees that overflow on to the sidewalks along the *quai* may represent an obstacle. Nevertheless, this is an idyllic spot for an early morning stroll.

The flower market occupies the Place Louis-Lépine, named after the turn-of-the-century Prefect of Police who first began regulating Paris traffic and who outfitted the *flics* with the snappy white gloves and white batons which since have become tradition. On Sundays the market changes its aspect completely. It is the one day of the week when the stalls shut down and the Marché aux Fleurs becomes the Marché aux Oiseaux, with thousands of chirping, squeaking, cooing, whistling and even talking birds. Many of them I suspect—like those fat, grey-white pigeons or those pretty little pheasants—will end up in a pot instead of a cage. The French, after all, could cook a parrot and make it taste delicious.

Considering that it is dignified with the spectacular solemnity of Notre-Dame and La Sainte-Chapelle, with the stern presence of the Palais de Justice and the grim relic of the Conciergerie, the old island of the Parisii remains the vibrant core of Paris. And nowhere is it more alive than down on the *quais*, the cobbled riverbanks where Paris is seen at her timeless best. Here, another part of the traditional fauna can be observed at its ancient rites: The *clochards*—the wine-soaked down-and-outers who have made their bargain with life heavy on the side of leisure—are sleeping in their rags, opening up cans of stew they have "borrowed" from unwary shops, cadging francs or sheltering under the bridges near a fisherman or two. In Anglo-Saxon countries such derelicts usually inspire fear, pity or loathing, but in Paris they are part of the community.

Once I walked by a group of three "*clodos*" and was thunderstruck to hear that they were discussing, between slugs of red wine, Diogenes and his search for truth. Another time a lone *clochard* won my attention and a franc with the news that it was the first day of spring and therefore *la Fête*

The rooftops of Paris, cluttered with dormer windows and jumbles of clay chimney pots, are one of the city's legendary visual attractions. But here on the Île de la Cité, two roof-menders (top), inured to the charm of their working environment, gaze instead at the Seine while taking a break from their job.

des Clochards. He had invented the holiday, of course, but it sounded impeccably logical—and in my book inventiveness like that is worth a franc any day. There are *clochard* men, *clochard* ladies and *clochard* couples; *clochard* soap-box orators, *clochard* barbers (my wife once saw a *clochard* lady shaving her gent on a park bench, spiffing him up for All Saints Day); part-time amateur *clochards*, who permit themselves to be photographed for a modest price, to be agreed in advance; and one rather ominous *clochard* "rat man", who has an act centring around a rubber rodent that he thrusts at unsuspecting bourgeois. *Clochards* are fine.

Upstream from the Marché aux Fleurs, behind Notre-Dame's spiderleg flying buttresses, is the footbridge leading to the "other island" of Paris: Île Saint-Louis. The perfect symmetry of this island's checker-board streets—almost the only part of Paris laid out in regular "blocks"—is an unmistakable sign that Île Saint-Louis was created artificially instead of mushrooming in the haphazard manner of the Cité or the Latin Quarter. This island was, in fact, Paris' first large-scale real-estate development. And here, too, as in so many aspects of the capital's life the original inspiration came from Henri IV, our friendly *Vert-Galant.*

More than 2,000 years ago, when the Parisii settled on the Île de la Cité they had no interest in the two smaller islands that lay to the east of it. The islets were known as the Île Notre-Dame and Île aux Vaches ("Cow Island"). For centuries, as the property of the monks of Notre-Dame, they remained generally unused, except for grazing cattle, holding religious fairs, training archers and from time to time, fighting duels. Henri IV finally approved a plan for developing the islands and when he was assassinated soon afterwards, it was left to his son, Louis XIII, to see the plan realized.

Louis XIII made the islands part of Paris by granting two entrepreneurs permission to fill in the channel between them and lay out the reclaimed land for housing. The project was completed shortly after 1650 and, curiously, it proved to be something of a failure. A few eccentric noblemen and parvenus chose the new quarter for building sumptuous *hôtels* (residences) and it attracted a number of *nouveaux riches*: merchants, bankers and magistrates. But not nearly enough people made the move to fulfil the promoters' ambitions, and they had no choice but to make the remaining plots smaller, build apartment houses instead of palaces and encourage the *petit peuple*—shopkeepers, artisans, even workers—to settle there.

The resulting Île Saint-Louis is linked to the Right Bank by three bridges and to the Left Bank by two. The main street, Rue St-Louis-en-l'Île, runs down the centre of the island and has a number of houses of unusual historic interest. At No. 12, at the turn of the 18th Century, Philippe Lebon introduced to the world the principle of gas lighting with a demonstration of his "Thermolamp". (He was mysteriously stabbed to death in the Champs-Élysées before the French government agreed to his plans for lighting up all of Paris.) No. 2 is the most opulent home on the island: the

Hôtel Lambert, where Voltaire and Jean-Jacques Rousseau lived—Voltaire with his mistress, Madame du Chatelet—and where Chopin was a regular guest. During the Second World War the Hôtel Lambert was the city's principal hide-out and transit point for Allied airmen shot down over France. ("*Louisiens*" were dour Resistance fighters and they take pride in having made their island the first district of Paris to be cleared of Germans in 1944.)

Physically, the island has hardly changed down through the years. But it is now the most exclusive and expensive neighbourhood in Paris; even those tiny apartments of the *petit peuple* are today virtually luxury residences. The beautiful Hôtel Lambert was bought by Guy de Rothschild when he gave up his family château, Ferrières. When a Rothschild gives up a château, he wants proper consolation.

The Île Saint-Louis has become a reserved and rather chilly museum, animated mostly by the presence of restaurants (usually bad) that proliferate there, and by the motorists vainly trying to discover available parking spots. It is only on the *quais*—and the river banks are especially beautiful here, broad and calm and lushly shaded by tall trees—that the blood and life of Paris show themselves again in the presence of the *clochards*, the card-players, the fishermen, the strollers and the *amoureux*.

In this respect, life on the Île Saint-Louis is unchanged. For hundreds of years, mavericks have congregated around its waterfronts; and it was here, at the end of the 18th Century, that the novelist Restif de la Bretonne became renowned for his curious mania for graffiti. Restif, a thoroughly unrepentant dirty old man, fell into the habit—and no one knows why—of inscribing his thoughts, observations and autobiographical anecdotes in Latin on the stone understructure of a bridge (which stood at the point of the present Pont de Sully). After five years, his elucubrations covered most of the lower part of the bridge and became a major attraction of the Île Saint-Louis. They are now, alas, gone, along with the bridge, but history has preserved most of the content. Two of my favourites are: *Abiit hodie monstrum* ("The Monster left today"), recording the day his wife deserted him; and *Data tota—felix* ("Gave herself entirely—happy"), marking his pleasure at the conquest of a young girl called Sara.

Restif de la Bretonne ("Of all the men of letters, I am the only one who frequents the lower classes") died in 1806. The citizens of Paris gave the king of graffiti a sumptuous funeral; his casket was followed by counts and countesses, university professors, politicians, workers and prostitutes. What better cross-section of the city's population could one hope for?

The Lazy, Much Beloved River

By the Right Bank's Quai de la Mégisserie, across the Seine from the Île de la Cité, Parisians enjoy their favourite river and the warmth of winter sunshine.

The River Seine holds the heart of Paris—and the hearts of Parisians—in its languorous embrace. Meandering in wide loops through and around the city, its shallow, slow-moving stream provides a sense of timeless peace that draws those seeking solace, recreation or romance. Strollers linger by its reflecting waters. Fishermen meditate at their lines. Lovers seek the discreet shadows of its 32 bridges or boldly demonstrate their affection on sunlit quays. Although Paris is France's third busiest port, the river never seems to bustle, its relaxed mood affecting even the crews working on freight barges. To Parisians, the Seine is too personal to be viewed merely as a commercial waterway; they prefer to hold it in reverence, as Napoleon did: "I wish my ashes to lie by the banks of the Seine," he wrote in his will, "in the heart of the nation that I loved so much."

Where the Seine skirts the Bois de Boulogne, Paris' huge park, a sunbathing man and dog, oblivious to passers-by, yield to the river's restful blandishments.

Spotlit by the summer sun, lovers lose themselves in a private rapture that—at least for a time—brings to life countless ballads about the Seine's magic.

Scarlet shirts and oar blades flash into the sunlight as a pair of two-man racing sculls speeds from the shadow of the Pont de Neuilly. This reach of the Seine, at the western, downriver suburb of Neuilly, is favoured by racing crews because of its generous width.

As their washing flaps in the breeze, a bargeman and his wife moor their craft in the heart of the city while their dog lounges on a cargo of builder's sand.

Two fishermen dangle lines, unconcerned about their possible catch. Most Paris anglers do not seek sport so much as they do a share of the river's tranquillity.

At Neuilly, on an old cargo barge that has been converted to a floating home, a group lingers over a midday meal in a commonplace affirmation of the ancient and still enduring love affair between Parisians and the Seine.

3

Life and Love on the Left Bank

Although the Left Bank of Paris is older than the Right Bank, it never quite grew up. The other side of the Seine—La Rive Droite, the Right Bank—with its commerce, money, power and elegance, is a place made for adults. La Rive Gauche, the Left Bank, has always managed to maintain an atmosphere of youth. It is the home of the Sorbonne and the Latin Quarter, the poets and artists of Montparnasse, and of the philosophers and Philistines of St-Germain des Prés. Even today, when the specializations of the ancient quarters tend to be blurred into modern uniformity, the student is still the real symbol of the Left Bank.

I am well aware of that symbol because I live near a venerable student hangout, Place St-Michel, a broad traffic-filled square by the Seine, opposite the old Royal Palace on the Île de la Cité. Hair length and clothing styles have changed since I was a student, but basically everything is the same as it always was. In the early days students used to congregate at a vineyard here; then came a jumble of medieval houses and inns. Now the pole of attraction is a huge, red marble fountain backed up against the wall of an old building that marks the bottom end of Boulevard St-Michel, the "high street" of the student quarter that runs south for about a mile. Any day of the year, winter or summer, young people gather around the curving parapet of the Fontaine St-Michel, as gregarious as the pigeons on the cornices above. Although they are often scruffy, the students offer a pleasingly disparate cocktail of racial types and languages. Sometimes they do a little amateur hustling ("*T'as pas cent balles?*" is the equivalent here of "Buddy, can you spare a dime?"). Sometimes they scratch guitars. Sometimes they just hang around and wait for things to happen. Are they all students at the Sorbonne? Who knows, but they are the right age— under 30. To one side of the fountain the edge of the square is lined with cafés, where endless cups of black coffee and glasses of beer, student drinks *par excellence*, are consumed day and night, always accompanied by the merry tintinabulation of the pinball machines.

The pinball machines deserve a digression. Like all the lovers kissing and fondling each other in public, the ubiquity of pinball machines, not just in the Latin Quarter but throughout much of Paris, often surprises the first-time visitor. Few cafés are without one or two of them, and they are almost always in use. The ironies of fate have decreed that the Gottlieb, the Rolls-Royce of *flippers* (as the French call the machines), is illegal in Chicago, where it is manufactured, but queen of Gay Paree. The French love for pinball is quite staggering; and the skilled, youthful Parisians must

On the sidewalk outside the Café des Deux Magots, chic customers relax in the spring sunshine as they observe the parade of Left Bank life on Boulevard St-Germain. The famous café got its name from two oriental figures (magots) on the sign of a Chinese silk shop that stood here in the 19th Century.

surely be the greatest players in the world. Watch a French student insouciantly pose his Gauloise on the thick glass of a "Fast Draw" or a "Shipmates", drive the steel ball into the jungle of bumpers, poppers, special score lanes and flanged score flags. Emotionless, his features as reposed as El Cordobes stalking in for the kill, he carefully guides the ball through the "500 when lit", whips it past the hazard of the side gate, rockets it obliquely two or three times off the taut trampoline of the side bumpers, then adeptly takes it on the tip of the flipper to propel it all the way to the top again. The best of them can play all afternoon on an initial investment of one franc, winning free game after game.

I have digressed too far. Let us go back to the beginning, to the 12th Century when Abélard defied the authority of Notre-Dame and led his followers from the Île de la Cité to the Left Bank. There were fields and gardens then in the vicinity of the present Place Maubert, and the students sat on bales of straw listening to lectures in the open air. Abélard and his fellow teachers were engaged mostly in the finer points of theology and logic. The freer flight of the liberal arts and sciences was still a long way off. But as the reputation of Paris scholarship grew, students flocked in from all sides, speaking all manner of strange languages and dialects. They followed the church's example and made Latin their common tongue, an act that gave rise to the name of the district: the Latin Quarter.

From the beginning the students had an uneasy relationship with the people already settled there. Between the thoughtless self-indulgence of youth and the *mauvais caractère* of the Parisians, sparks were bound to fly. In fact, the University of Paris itself, the Left Bank's most characteristic institution, began—how very Parisian!—because of a fight. This historic brawl occurred in the Year of Grace 1200. The circumstances have not come down to us in detail, but apparently the servant of a German student got drunk, and presumably rowdy, in a local inn. Parisians have never been overly tolerant of each other, and are even less so of foreigners and their lackeys. The innkeeper roundly thrashed the German valet and the students retaliated by marching *en bande* to the alehouse and giving the publican what-for. The presumptuousness (*étrangers* laying hands on the local tavern keeper!) raised public indignation to such a pitch that a *prévôt*, a sheriff named Thomas, led all the population he could round up to the Germans' lodgings and took the place by storm. Town-gown relations were at a low point indeed; five students died in the battle.

Welded into dramatic solidarity, the entire teaching and student corps now demanded justice from King Philippe-Auguste. After reviewing the facts, the king threw the sheriff and his accomplices into a dungeon, officially recognized the existence of the corporation of masters and students, and promised that henceforth they would be answerable only to ecclesiastical justice—the first major steps towards the self-governing

In a small bar just off Boulevard St-Germain, a couple indulge in a favourite Parisian pastime—the public embrace—and their images are replicated in a mirrored door (right). Their demonstrative passion is totally ignored by a pair of players, equally absorbed, intent on a pinball game (les flippers), also a perennial craze among the city's young.

liberal community that the university was to become. Already it had its own language; now it had its own law, the teachers and students being exempt from civil jurisdiction and answerable only to the Church. Fifteen years later, Pope Innocent III, who had himself studied under Abélard, authorized the corporation in his turn and the University of Paris was now officially recognized by name.

Recognition did not bring total acceptance, however, and down through the years conflicts between local inhabitants and the students raged on. But in spite of setbacks (at one point the students protested the cruel methods used to suppress their rioting by leaving town for six years), the university grew into a thriving and influential community. The name by which it became known—the Sorbonne—was originally that of one *collège* where poor students could come to learn with a real roof over their heads, and sit on a wooden floor rather than on bales of hay as in Abélard's day. From its modest beginnings that establishment became the richest and most respected of all the colleges in Paris. It could boast such celebrated teachers as St. Thomas Aquinas and Roger Bacon, such brilliant students as Dante, Erasmus and St. Ignatius de Loyola. Its founder, the cleric, Robert de Sorbon, gave his name by extension to the entire university.

As time passed, the original theology and logic made way for other studies, notably the arts known as liberal: grammar, rhetoric, dialectic, arithmetic, geometry, astronomy and music. Thanks to the university, Paris became the new Athens, the most important intellectual centre of medieval Christianity—even if the students stubbornly maintained their reputation for womanizing, gluttony and laziness. For almost 700 years Latin continued to be the language of the Latin Quarter—right up to the Revolution, when the university, seen as a stronghold of reaction, was shut down. Napoleon opened it up again in 1806, with French now the mandatory language.

I am ashamed to admit that I never got into any fights with the townspeople during my student year in Paris, and that I further dishonoured the Sorbonne's glorious traditions by engaging in only the mildest of gluttony (the student restaurants didn't encourage it) and scarcely any womanizing. Only in laziness did I bear the old torch high, properly neglecting my studies for the joys of discovering Paris and the French. *Flâner*—meaning to hang around, stroll, walk from place to place with no purpose other than looking and enjoying—is what I did. At the Sorbonne, one is ideally placed to be a *flâneur*.

Close by, for instance, is one of the magic areas of the Left Bank: the Rue de la Huchette-Rue St-Séverin quarter. This tangled maze of little, medieval lanes is one of the oldest parts of Paris, and yet everything about it is youthful. Like a medieval fair brought up-to-date for the 20th Century, it is crowded with strollers (the whole section has wisely been closed to traffic), singers, musicians, and sometimes even jugglers and fire-eaters.

All around there is a lively jumble of little shops, cinemas, bars and dives; and the air is filled with intriguing smells emitting from exotic restaurants—Chinese, Italian, Greek, Arab, Japanese and even (quite rare in this area) one or two that are French.

Down at the far end of Rue de la Huchette, cutting through a block of buildings towards the Seine, is the alleyway with my favourite street name, Rue du Chat-qui-Pêche (Street of the Fishing Cat), and just around the corner is the Petit Pont, occupying the site of one of the two Roman bridges of Lutèce. Near by is the oldest tree in all Paris: a fragile, false acacia brought over from Guinea in the early 17th Century and planted in the shadow of the ancient university church of St-Julien-le-Pauvre. It is now the most pampered and carefully attended tree in a city that defends its trees (3,500 are replaced every year) with the kind of passion that some people reserve for cats and dogs. The church itself is among the oldest of the city's landmarks. The present structure dates back to the 12th Century.

In the other direction, south-west from the Sorbonne, are the Luxembourg Gardens, which can easily use up a *flâneur's* afternoon on any but the most hideously unpleasant and rainy of days. When I first wandered in, I vaguely knew that the big edifice at the foot of the park which now houses the French Senate (that rubber-toothed legislative bulldog) had originally been the palace of Marie de' Medici, Henri IV's queen, but that didn't especially interest me. What excited me was what always excites me about French parks—they are so beautiful, so clean and so full of pleasures, and they are well protected. Parisian parks like the Luxembourg are surrounded by tall and stout wrought-iron barricades set in stone at the bottom and as sharp as spears at the top. Gates permit them to be closed at night, and the late-afternoon whistles of the guards—eerie, distant trillings among the trees—signal that daylight is waning and it is time to get out. People leave without protest. After all, who would want to remain in a park overnight, unless for sinister purpose? The French simply cannot understand the drugs problems, the knifings and rapings in American parks at night.

The smartly uniformed guards, whom a stranger might mistake for police, open the Luxembourg gates at first light for the joggers, the early dog-walkers and the inevitable stream of office workers who use the park as a short-cut. Shortly after, the mothers and the nannies arrive with their baby carriages, and then come the *flâneurs* like me. If it is summer, the mothers and children make a beeline for the octagonal pond in the centre where youngsters launch their sailing boats in the light puffs of wind that breeze down the hill from the Avenue de l'Observatoire. There is a place for everything in the park: miles of intriguingly curved and landscaped paths for promenading, an old stone-and-wrought-iron bandstand for concerts, a few tennis courts, a marionette theatre (starring the

Two Thousand Years of Turbulent Change

3rd Century B.C.	Parisii tribesmen already living on Île de la Cité, in a settlement called Lutèce
53 B.C.	Julius Caesar's Roman troops occupy the island and call it Lutetia
c. A.D. 285	St-Denis (first bishop of Paris) is one of many early Christians martyred at Montmartre by Romans
c. 305	A milestone records first known reference to Lutetia as "Paris" (from Parisii)
451	Ste-Geneviève is credited with saving city from invading Huns by the power of her prayers
5th Century	Germanic Barbarians establish sway over Western Roman Empire
508	Clovis, king of the Franks, makes Paris his capital
8th Century	Paris declines in political importance after Charlemagne moves his court to Aix-la-Chapelle
888	Franks elect Odo, Count of Paris, king of France after his successful defence of Paris against marauding Normans
987	Hugh Capet elected king of France; founds Capetian dynasty with Paris as its capital
1115	Influential theologian Pierre Abélard begins teaching in cathedral school of Notre-Dame
1163	Construction of Notre-Dame cathedral begins
1190	King Philippe-Auguste orders construction of Louvre fortress and new walls around Paris
1215	Pope Innocent III officially recognizes University of Paris, previously a loose association of schools
1248	Building of La Sainte-Chapelle to house holy relics is completed for Louis IX (St-Louis)
1253	Robert de Sorbon founds Sorbonne College at University of Paris
1348	Black Death reaches Paris; two-thirds of Europe's population die as result of the plague
1357-8	Unsuccessful anti-royalist rebellion in Paris under Étienne Marcel, dean of the Merchants' Guild, a powerful civic organization. Court moves from Île de la Cité to the Louvre on Right Bank

1364-83	Charles V builds new walls around expanded city and constructs the Bastille
1419	Feuding factions among the French invite the English to occupy Paris. Duke of Bedford takes possession of the city
1431	Henry VI of England crowned king of France in Notre-Dame
1436	French forces of King Charles VII recapture Paris
1534	Ignatius Loyola founds Society of Jesus in Paris
1572	St. Bartholomew's Day massacre of Huguenots in struggles between Catholics and Protestants
1588	Day of the Barricades; Catholics turn against Henri III, forcing him to flee Paris
1594	Henri IV gains control of Paris after conversion to Catholicism
1610	Henri IV assassinated by a Catholic fanatic, Ravaillac
1643	Accession of Louis XIV, the Sun King (so-called for the brilliance of his court)
1670	City fortifications demolished and replaced by boulevards
1678-82	Louis XIV transfers his court to magnificent new palace at Versailles
c. 1760	Place de la Concorde and Church of Ste-Geneviève (Panthéon) are constructed
1789	Outbreak of French Revolution: Parisians storm the Bastille, symbol of monarchical repression
1793	Louis XVI (nominally king until 1792) is guillotined
1793-4	The Terror: struggling revolutionary factions send Royalists and each other to the guillotine
1804	Napoleon crowns himself emperor in Notre-Dame
1815	Battle of Waterloo. Monarchy is restored under Louis XVIII
1848	Revolution in Paris deposes Louis-Philippe as liberal movement sweeps Europe
1853-70	Baron Haussmann, Prefect under Napoleon III, orders radical reconstruction of the city to improve its amenities and make it easier to police
1870	Franco-Prussian war, over rivalry for European leadership. Parisians starve under siege
1871	In aftermath of Franco-Prussian war, Paris is briefly governed by socialist commune
1889	Eiffel Tower is completed
1900	Basilica of Sacré-Coeur is built on Butte Montmartre. First line of Métro railway opened
1914	First World War: Paris under threat of German attack is saved by the Battle of the Marne
1919	Treaty of Versailles
1940	Second World War: city is surrendered to Germans
1944	Allied forces liberate Paris. General de Gaulle becomes head of provisional government
1951	Paris celebrates 2000th anniversary of the founding of Roman Lutetia
1958	De Gaulle is elected first president of the Fifth Republic
1968	Students and workers protest against social and economic conditions with violent demonstrations and strikes
1969	De Gaulle resigns and is succeeded by Georges Pompidou who promotes construction of new skyscrapers and roads in Paris. Paris' wholesale food market leaves Les Halles for suburban Rungis
1974	Giscard d'Estaing is elected president and institutes anti-highrise conservationist policy for the city

famous Guignol character), terraces crowded with statues of French queens and famous women, a playground full of swings, a couple of sandboxes, even a beehive, complete with honey.

Everything in the park is so well ordered that the children even play carefully, hardly smudging their faces or dirtying their clothes. In America, I had been accustomed to wild, unruly kids whose play was just one notch this side of apocalypse. The orderliness of French children disconcerted me, and it still does. But it does not surprise me anymore: it is the French way. Only verbally are they allowed to release their latent aggressiveness: they will shout the most horrible threats at each other, but unlike the hunchbacked Polichinelle, whom they see thumping his wife with a big stick at the marionette theatre, they rarely come to blows.

The students of the Sorbonne continue to use the Luxembourg benches, as they have done for centuries, for the pursuit of reading and of each other. In the opposite direction from the university, to the east, lies another quarter they favour just as much: Rue Mouffetard, popularly known as "La Mouffe". To reach "La Mouffe" from the Sorbonne you must pass the Panthéon, and while this edifice with its absurd bulk and monstrously large dome has little attraction for Parisian students or for me, it does bring to mind the legend of Ste-Geneviève, Paris' patron saint. In A.D. 451 Attila the Hun, known to his pals as the Scourge of God, was marching across Gaul with his barbarian hordes. A few weeks earlier they had reduced Cologne to ashes, reportedly ravishing 11,000 virgins while they were at it, and now they were burning a fire-path towards Paris. The Romans packed up and left, but a young woman named Geneviève exhorted the Parisians to stay, assuring them that she knew God was on their side and would divert the barbarians.

At the eleventh hour the locusts of Attila suddenly changed direction, sparing Paris and swooping instead on Orléans (where, ironically, the Roman administration had retreated for safety). Student wits maintain that Attila bypassed Paris when he learned it was the last place on earth to look for 11,000 virgins. But the Parisians of the 5th Century credited the miracle to Geneviève.

Hailed as a saint, and officially recognized by the church in 1330, Geneviève became an immortal protectress whose divine intervention saved Paris again and again, including during the First World War, when—it is said—she drove the Germans away from the city. The steepest hill in the Latin Quarter was named for her, and it has been called Montagne-Ste-Geneviève ever since. In the 18th Century, Louis XV built a church there dedicated to Ste-Geneviève, which has since become the Panthéon, a national memorial to France's illustrious dead.

Rue Mouffetard, a few hundred yards from the Panthéon, is one of the oldest streets in Paris, being the relic of the old Roman *via* that led to

Lyon. It has tiny theatres, shops and boutiques, flower pedlars and a few of the old *petits métiers* craftsmen, like glasscutters and knife-sharpeners. Above all, it has the Mouffetard market, so varied and crowded and colourful that it makes up a miniature world of its own. Here every small trader has his own act, and some—like the fishmonger near the bottom of the hill who ends his performance with a robust lobster sitting on top of his head—draw fans from all over the city.

"La Mouffe" is relatively modern now, with running water and electricity and a municipal sewage system, but its medieval atmosphere remains and, within the extraordinary swirl and din of the crowds, it is easy to imagine the animation of Paris' streets in the Middle Ages. Even without automobiles, the streets were no less noisy then. They were also dangerously filthy, with the open sewer trench running down the middle to receive all of society's leavings, from fish guts to the contents of chamber pots that were merrily emptied from upper storeys with the cry: "*Gare à l'eau!*—Watch out for the water!" Furthermore, there was scarcely any room for pedestrians to move freely because tradesmen encroached on the public street when they opened their stalls in the early morning. Voices ricochetted in a permanent babble among the narrow spaces between the houses, and even at night there was never complete silence because the trade signs of wood and metal would swing and creak in the gentlest breeze. Old Parisian signs (you can still see many of them at the little Carnavalet Museum on the Right Bank) were remarkably numerous and varied. To catch the eye, tradesmen made them as big and as dramatic as possible. Here a toothpuller displayed a molar the size of an armchair; near by a tavern named *La Bonne Femme*, was pointedly identified by a huge cut-out of a woman without a head. The interminable squeaking and grinding of these signs swinging on their iron poles brought so many complaints from insomniacs that, in the 18th Century, they were outlawed in favour of paintings and bas-reliefs on the façades above the merchants' shops. There are still a few of these in "La Mouffe".

By now you will have grasped my perverse prejudice in favour of the Paris street life and the *petit peuple*—what W. B. Yeats called "the blood and mire of humanity"—and my relative opacity to the charms of many a magnificent monument. So it will come as no surprise that, when I took up permanent residence in Paris, I chose for my first apartment an artist's *atelier* in a curious, off-beat section of town near the Porte d'Orléans. My studio was in a quiet, shaded courtyard that opened on to Rue de la Tombe-Issoire, the street of Issoire's tomb, another of my favourite names. Locals explained to me that Issoire, a corruption of the name Isoré, was a mean and mythical king of the Saracens, a giant 15 feet tall who set up camp on the hill known as Montmartre and strode up to the gates of Paris every morning crying out his challenge for a champion to come

True to their traditional attitude of defiance, banner-waving students sing out protests against French educational and political policies in Place de la Bastille, a public square historically associated with demonstrations against unpopular rule. The 169-foot-high July Column commemorates those who died during the revolts of 1830 and 1848.

A Menagerie of Signs

A picturesque legacy of Paris' commercial past are the animal effigies many traders still use as symbols. The tradition is so strong that some enterprises have adopted such signs although there is no apparent relationship between the business being conducted and the chosen emblem: for example, the monkey (bottom row, right) decorates a shop selling lamps and antiques.

Usually, however, the messages conveyed by the zoo of figures are straightforward. A snail (middle row, left) marks a restaurant specializing in escargots. A boar (middle row, centre) lures customers to a pork butcher. A dragon (bottom row, centre) is simply the street sign for Rue du Dragon, and a turtle (bottom row, second from left) clings to a shop that sells tortoiseshell objects. Some are reminders of bygone days. A civet cat (top row, left) identifies a tobacconist, probably because the musk of civet cats once was used to flavour tobacco.

out and fight. Finally, so legend has it, he was killed in my street by one Guillaume d'Orange who used an extra-long sharp blade to reach up and slit the oaf's throat.

Plenty of artists have lived near the scene of this David and Goliath combat. Until his death in 1965 it wasn't unusual to see the sculptor Alberto Giacometti, as tall and gaunt as one of his statues, stalking across the junction of Rue de la Tombe-Issoire and Rue d'Alésia. But the two local residents who fascinated me most were not artists at all—and they were long since dead and gone when I arrived there. They were Lenin and the Nameless Old Man.

My friend Mario Ruspoli, a film maker, first told me the tragic and shameful tale of *la pissotière de Lénine*. In the old days (before women's liberation accelerated their decline) the *pissotière*, or public urinal, was a great Paris institution—a green-painted relief station to be found as readily and handily as a telephone booth. And, Lenin's *pissotière*—so called because the Great Man himself often used it during his time of exile before the October Revolution—was located in the middle of a minuscule square little more than a stone's throw from my courtyard off Rue de la Tombe-Issoire.

The distinguished patronage of this people's convenience was confirmed by the old gentleman who used to run a combined grocery store and bar at one corner of the square. "Ah, *Monsieur Lénine*. He was a fine man. A bit serious though. He preferred white wine, you know. And when he was through he used to go right over there." Proudly, he gestured towards the *pissotière*.

Our comfort station held its own echoes of history, then, but that was not its only distinction. It was not just one of those commonplace round *pissoirs* where customers stood all around with backs to the outer wall. Nor was it one of those graciously styled *triplace* types, shaped like clover leaves. This was that rarest of Paris *pissoirs*: a *biplace*, where gentlemen stood facing each other across a protective partition beneath an overhang of translucent glass, and often conversed.

The irreparable and tragic crime was committed one autumn night in 1974. Following orders, three municipal employees, acting swiftly and ruthlessly, drove up with a crane truck and steel-cutting acetylene torches and unceremoniously plucked Lenin's *pissotière* out of Rue de la Tombe-Issoire and carried it away to the municipal scrapheap. As a result, the taxi drivers at the near-by cab-rank have ever since had nowhere convenient to go. It would serve the Paris city council right if they all grew embittered and turned communist. Lenin would be properly avenged. Worse still, we are forever denied the simple diversion of standing at the same *biplace* and imagining what footnotes to history might have been exchanged across the partition in Lenin's day.

The Nameless Old Man was not of the same illustrious stature as Lenin.

When this photograph was taken during the 1940s, the iron-walled pissoir was a commonplace of Paris streets. In recent years, municipal authorities have gradually been removing these distinctive conveniences.

However, he was a real Parisian, this fellow, always dissatisfied. I learned about him because he had once owned the *atelier* in which I was living. In his retirement, with plenty of time on his hands, he decided one day that he would dig himself a cellar. After all, what is a *résidence* without a *cave*? For months and months the neighbours could hear his patient, mole-like progress as he attacked the soil beneath his home and brought up buckets of sandy earth that he dumped in the garbage cans outside. The old man got his cellar all right, but he went a few feet too far and had the shock of his life when he punched through to an underground chamber and found himself with a private entrance to the catacombs of Paris. He had the biggest *cave* in town, but the sight of all those human skulls grinning back at him was too much; he cemented up the opening and abandoned his cellar. By the time I took over the apartment his basement was just a bleak hole, full of old boards, broken furniture and empty bottles, and infested with rats and spiders. I never ventured down there.

Perhaps I should have been more adventurous. Since then I have learned that the catacombs of Paris are amazingly extensive. They occupy a tiny proportion of the uncounted miles of stone quarries that have lain under the city since Roman times. The limestone and gypsum (used for making plaster of Paris) is so rich in quality and quantity that the city was built by simply digging straight down to obtain construction materials. The first open-pit quarries soon gave way to high-domed mines and, when these had been exhausted, they were abandoned. Unfortunately, no one at the time troubled to map the hidden chasms; and as the city expanded over the centuries, the mines were forgotten and whole quarters were erected over them. Seepage water gradually ate away the pits (lime is soluble in water) until there was no support left for the buildings above. Disaster followed. In the mid-18th Century Paris literally began to collapse. Only then was the problem of the quarries taken seriously. The city authorities began mapping the underground, filling water-dissolved pits with earth and rubble, and sealing off mine entrances. By 1813 all stone-mining was forbidden within the city; and by 1860, around the city limits as well.

Nevertheless, the vast network of tunnels and caverns continued to have their uses—as lairs for thieves and cut-throats, as hideouts for revolutionaries, rebels, and soldiers in time of war (the catacombs became the nerve-centre of the Resistance movement in 1944), as "farms" for mushroom-growers (the famous mushrooms, *champignons de Paris*, are so named because they were first grown in the quarries). Near the foundations of the Val-de-Grâce Hospital (not far from the Sorbonne) there is a monument to the memory of one Philibert Aspairt, who wandered a bit too far downstairs in 1793 and was not discovered—in skeleton form—until 1804. Early in the 20th Century, workers passing through a quarry beneath the Odéon area came upon a baffling cat cemetery—hundreds and hundreds of feline skeletons. Did alley cats, they wondered, have some graveyard instinct like elephants, some distant racial memory that impelled them to totter down to this boneyard when they felt death approaching? The explanation was simpler. Above them was a sealed-up, obsolete well that years before had stood in the courtyard of a restaurant famous for its *fricassées* of "wild hare".

It is possible to make a conducted tour of one section of the catacombs of Paris, entering them from No. 2, Place Denfert-Rochereau, not far from the northern end of Rue de la Tombe-Issoire. This is a gruesome experience that I can hardly recommend. Armed with a torch, you descend a spiral staircase that leads on to a great labyrinth of galleries lined with thousands of human bones and skulls. Here is a vast charnel-house reputed to contain the remains of nearly three million people, skeletons dating from around 1785 when it became the dumping-ground for bones taken from disused graveyards and for many of those executed in the Revolution. And this eerie place represents no more than a tenth of the Paris underground system. In all, it is estimated that the remains of at least six million people lie beneath the city.

Believe it or not, a tour of these catacombs became highly fashionable at the start of the 19th Century. An emperor of Austria and later Napoleon III both made the *tour de mort* with much ceremony and—on April Fools' Day, 1897—exercising a most macabre sense of humour, a group of musicians descended to the ossuary to give a concert to the gallery of dry bones. Perhaps, after all, it would be more fitting if everyone heeded the inscription at the main entrance to the catacombs. In

the words of the 18th-Century poet Jacques Delille, it reads: "Stop! This is the realm of the dead."

Two massive stone buildings house this entrance and the offices of the *inspection-générale* of quarries, and they are of historical interest in themselves as reminders of one of the most ingenious fund-raising tricks ever devised by a finance minister. In the 18th Century a group of royal tax collectors, known as *fermiers-généraux*, farmers-general, enforced their hold over Paris by building a wall around the city. The great wall was not for defensive purposes, but to ensure that all commerce in and out of the city passed through their avaricious hands by way of the *barrières*: ornamented toll-gates that they set up at strategic points. The Denfert-Rochereau buildings are among the few *barrières* still standing, now that tax collectors have found more refined means of extorting money.

From my *atelier* off Rue de la Tombe-Issoire, I always enjoyed the walk northwards, past the shops and markets of Avenue du Général-Leclerc, past the big, dopy lion statue at Place Denfert-Rochereau and on down Boulevard Raspail to the intersection of Montparnasse. Artists' *ateliers* proliferate around this area, some of them miserable little unheated hutches, others positively sumptuous, the residences of *gros bourgeois* who enjoy playing at bohemian life. Jean-Paul Sartre, so long identified with St-Germain des Prés, eventually settled here on Boulevard Raspail, in an apartment only a hundred yards from Simone de Beauvoir's, their intellectual symbiosis only enhanced by their status as a separate but equal couple. From time to time, I would pass The Master in the street, or in the Café Raspail Vert, hunched over his *café-crème* and *croissants*. "Mornin', J.P." He never looked up from *l'Humanité*.

Likely as not, my destination in those days was La Coupole on Boulevard du Montparnasse—the busiest restaurant in France and the most interesting, too. I mention it here, rather than in my later chapter on gastronomy, because it is a sociological phenomenon as much as a restaurant. The food is respectable enough, considering that the kitchen serves close on 2,000 meals a day, but that is not the attraction. It is the people and the atmosphere that make La Coupole the most popular restaurant in town. Just as much as the Eiffel Tower and Notre-Dame, it is a landmark; and to come to Paris without visiting it would be a cultural irresponsibility.

La Coupole occupies the site of a former coal depot, within a few yards' walk of three famous Montparnasse cafés: the Dôme, the Rotonde, and the Select. It eclipsed all its rivals right from its opening night (December 20, 1927), when several of its first clients decided that it would be prudent to crawl home on hands and knees, "because of the icy road conditions". René Laffont, the perspicacious founder, had his finger on the pulse of Montparnasse and created in La Coupole a bohemian forum, a meeting place where freaks and prudes could share neutral ground and observe

Resembling a skeletal, gold-plated beetle, a sculpture is transported to a Paris gallery on top of the artist's motor car. The surreal ensemble had the shock effect that Left Bank artists have always desired: it served to attract some attention in the blasé city.

each other. His stroke of genius was to arrange a labyrinth of benches and tables through which arriving customers had to parade as if on exhibition.

Everyone sees everyone else at La Coupole. That is half the reason for going there. It is like a visit to the zoo. As the army of waiters skilfully threads between the tables bearing colossal trays of *cassoulet, choucroute garnie* and *fruits de mer*, the most astonishing cross-section of Parisiana shuffles forward to its traditional seating: artists and freaks on the left, the bourgeois on the right. Just about everybody who is somebody in France has been to La Coupole at one time or another. Giscard d'Estaing went there when he was Finance Minister; Hemingway hung out there; and Gertrude Stein and Henry Miller and James Joyce. Salvador Dali gave at least two canvasses to the head waiter. Josephine Baker appeared there half naked, with an ocelot on a leash. Other ladies have displayed themselves there without either ocelot or clothes. La Coupole is a grand institution.

I find it intriguing how strongly, almost indelibly, certain parts of Paris become identified with certain functions and styles of living. Just as St-Michel and the Montagne-Ste-Geneviève have been regarded for many centuries as essentially student areas, so Boulevard du Montparnasse will always be associated with artists—or more precisely, with painters, poets and novelists. There has been more high-quality artistic endeavour on and around that long, wide and busy street than on any other thoroughfare in the world. To this vicinity came such rising giants as Picasso, Rodin, Braque. Some were merely passing through; some, like Modigliani, were literally starving to death there; some—like Baudelaire, Maupassant, Saint-Saëns and Sainte-Beuve—were destined to remain there forever, in the Montparnasse Cemetery.

Around 1900, Montparnasse came into its own as artists began flooding into it. Soon the whole Paris school was there: Derain, Vlaminck, Modigliani, Kisling, Mondrian, Lipchitz, Soutine, Chagall, Léger. What a crowd! The Douanier Rousseau had been there before them. The poets of Montparnasse were Paul Fort and Apollinaire; they drew inspiration from their earlier and even more illustrious *compères*: Verlaine, Rimbaud and Baudelaire—the "damned" poets, singers of decadence and melancholy.

The Montparnasse spirit—sometimes frenetically joyful, sometimes depressed and close to madness, and always quick to shock the bourgeois, was first personified by that strange, tortured, enigmatic genius, the poet Gérard de Nerval. Nerval left a considerable body of work behind him, including a classic translation of *Faust*, but he was no slouch on gestures, either. He dumbfounded plenty of honest burghers by walking down Montparnasse with a lobster on a leash; and he chose the place of his death with rueful, humoristic precision, hanging himself in 1855 from a wrought-iron grille at the corner of Slaughter Street (Rue de la Tuerie) and the Impasse—a blind alley, or dead end street—of the Old Lanterne (Impasse de la Vieille Lanterne).

Montparnasse even had its influence on the false decadents of the American "Lost Generation"—making Hemingway, Dos Passos, Fitzgerald and MacLeish a little less boy-scoutish. One of the most colourful of this group's characters was Arthur Cravan, a muscular giant and poor writer who claimed to be related to Oscar Wilde. Cravan also claimed to be a prizefighter of world class and in 1916 talked himself into a match with Jack Johnson, who might just have been the greatest heavyweight fighter of all time. Cravan was flattened in the first round and didn't talk much about boxing after that.

By this time Lenin had left the Montparnasse area, as had Trotsky and the novelist Ilya Ehrenburg. But their memory lingered on: every time she got in her cups, a black prostitute named Aicha complained that Lenin, even after he made it to the top, never bothered to pay her back the money he owed her. The bum.

Today it has become fashionable to say that Montparnasse is "finished" (nothing is ever what it used to be) in terms of intellectual or bohemian life. Yet, there is still an aura of special excitement and activity about the place. It cannot be simply the low rents of its working-class tenements and *ateliers* that attracted so many kindred, creative spirits to the region. Paris had other cheap-living quarters. But Montparnasse has something more, some indefinable magic that spurred creativity. Even its name is a creation, an early literary joke. For centuries there was a large and imposing pile of gravel and rubble there, a quarry tip overgrown with weeds and shrubbery, favoured by students from the Latin Quarter as an ideal spot for extramural wenching, boozing and declaiming bad poetry. As a self-deprecating gag, they called the place Mount Parnassus, after the hallowed Greek peak that was the home of the Muses and the favourite spot for the orgies of worshippers of Dionysus, god of wine. The name stuck, and it became officially adopted when the present trace of the boulevard was laid out in the early 19th Century.

If Montparnasse stands for art, St-Germain des Prés, to its north, stands for philosophy, song and jazz. *Prés* means meadows, and originally this was a little suburban village—a *bourg*—that grew up around an old church outside the city walls. The village was soon annexed to the burgeoning municipality, but it always retained a charm and identity of its own. After the Second World War it became identified with philosophers and intellectuals largely because of Jean-Paul Sartre (then living in Rue de Seine) and his Kierkegaard-inspired theories that went by the name of Existentialism. In reality, Montparnasse-style thinkers and creators had been frequenting its old streets long before Sartre arrived.

As far back as the 17th Century, foreign painters—Italian, Flemish and German—congregated in Bourg St-Germain because they could sell their works freely without being restricted by the laws of Paris (within the city, only the protectionist guild of Parisian painters was allowed to carry

When these photographs were taken at the turn of the century, the streets of Paris were a vast outdoor workshop, full of people busily earning their livings. Most were self-employed, pursuing their "petits métiers" (little trades) wherever they could find customers. Today's economy curtails such independence, but picturesque tradesmen, self-employed or not, have not entirely vanished (see following page).

A Left Bank knife grinder.

A street sweeper cleaning cobbles.

A "washer of dogs" by the Seine.

An organ grinder and a singer.

on commerce). Gauguin and Rodin lurked around the Odéon, the square east of the church, and Eugène Delacroix had his studio in the perfect little jewel that is Place Furstenberg, lending his talents, among other enterprises, to the decoration of a chapel in old St-Sulpice. Such disparate types as Wagner, Stendhal and Apollinaire lived in the neighbourhood; Anatole France was born there, Racine and Oscar Wilde died there; and the arts-and-crafts influence still lingers on in its cafés, bookshops, antiquaries, and in the dozens of minuscule art galleries whose owners somehow manage to eke out a part-time living.

In fostering intellectual and artistic life, the cafés of St-Germain des Prés served as a lightning-rod, just as they did in Montparnasse. For those who care about counting such social points (*le standing*, as the French say), there are only three establishments that really matter at St-Germain: the Café de Flore, the Deux Magots and the Brasserie Lipp. They were all bursting with excitement in the late '40s and early '50s, when the constraints of German occupation were finally over and Parisians were able to talk openly again, to drink and dance, to make noise and love and music as they had been longing to do ever since the lights went out in 1940. Sartre, Genet and Simone de Beauvoir seemed to be more partial to the Flore, but André Breton, poet and self-proclaimed founder of surrealism, and a host of other lively spirits were next door at the Deux Magots. Across Boulevard St-Germain, at the Brasserie Lipp an iron-willed *maître d'hôtel* was introducing a subtle yet devastating form of discrimination that still applies to customers today: if you are important, you are seated on the ground floor; if you are a nobody, a table can always be found for you on the next floor up.

It was in the vaulted stone caves of St-Germain, in clubs like the Tabou, the Saint-Colombier and the Rose-rouge, that Boris Vian and Juliette Gréco threw their acid songs at the bourgeois who loved the insults and came back for more. And it was here that questionable but enthusiastic French adaptations of Dixieland ruined a million nights' sleep until the first discotheques came along to institutionalize group callisthenics.

St-Germain des Prés is still there today, but like everything else it has changed—and not for the better in my judgment. The mania for transmogrifying authentic French bistros into plywood English pubs has gripped otherwise sensible *commerçants*, and trivial boutiques have sprung up in such numbers I wonder how long a mere handful of streets can go on supporting them. At the same time, it is certainly true that the area is more animated than ever. After fighting their way through some of the most redoubtable traffic on earth, the intellectuals still gather on the terrace of the Deux Magots, now reading *le Monde* instead of Kierkegaard. The male clients of the Flore—young men with the eyes of fawns and the silky movements of gazelles—are as numerous as ever. At the corner of St-Germain and Rue de Rennes, pretty little boys with mean, professional eyes and

Today there are relatively few self-employed artisans, genuine followers of "petits métiers", in the city. Most workers are on payrolls and most work is done indoors. But while their jobs may not qualify as "petits métiers", there are still plenty of craftsmen, identifiable by their costumes or products, who provide colourful and lively reminders of the old tradition.

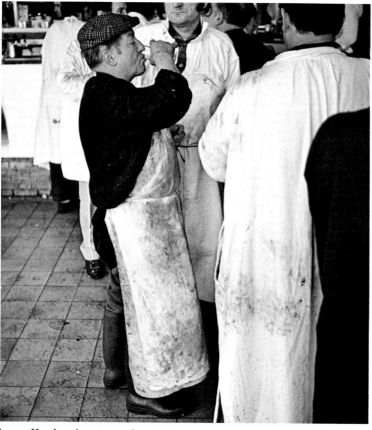

In a café, a butcher sips a glass of wine.

Sparks fly from a knife grinder's wheel.

A furniture maker carries a chair frame.

Glaziers deliver their wares on their backs.

pouting lips lean against the wall by *le Drugstore* while awaiting customers. As for the rest of business here, I believe it was Balzac who once said he was afraid that the world would some day be taken over by hairdressers. They have a pretty good bridgehead around St-Germain des Prés.

Although I like to regard the Left Bank as being more human and artistic than it is monumental, two of the greatest of all Parisian monuments stand on this side of the river: the Eiffel Tower and Les Invalides. The former, bestriding the Champs-de-Mars between the École Militaire and the Seine, is one of the most famous structures in the world, a work of mathematical genius that is a magnet to around three million visitors every year (double the number who flock to the Louvre) and far and away the greatest tourist attraction in all France.

Gustave Eiffel, an engineer and inventor who was an authentic genius, swept aside 700 rivals in the competition to design the *pièce de résistance* of the 1889 International Exposition marking the centenary of the start of the French Revolution. With his stupendous Tour Eiffel he quite literally pushed the use of iron in construction to new heights: 984 feet. It was increased to 1,051 feet in 1957 when a television tower and antenna were added. It was the tallest structure on earth for 41 years until surpassed by the Chrysler Building in New York.

Yet its progress to its present prestige was by no means smooth and uneventful. When building began in 1887, an angry horde of artists and traditionalists denounced the planned intrusion into the Paris skyline, and the protest petition of 300 well-known figures included the names of Gounod, Dumas, Huysmans, de Maupassant and Charles Garnier, architect of the Opéra. Among printable insults heaped upon the enterprise were "a hollow candlestick" . . . "arrogant ironmongery" . . . "a solitary suppository". In 1909 it was due to be demolished and was only saved because it provided the best aerial for the new-fangled science of wireless telegraphy. All objections to that reprieve were finally silenced in 1914, when the Eiffel Tower station picked up details of a German attack on Paris and so enabled the French military to be strategically placed for the first battle of the Marne.

Since then the tower has figured in a thousand-and-one true life dramas and curious incidents. It has been threatened by terrorists' explosives, "sold" innumerable times to gullible foreigners, and once (during the years 1925 to 1936) it underwent the supreme indignity of serving as the world's largest electric advertising billboard, its entire turret from the second landing to the top being blazoned by 250,000 lamps that made up the name CITROËN in six colours. Bicyclists have ridden down its 1,792 steps; at least one elephant has walked up them; alpinists have scaled its girdered face; and more than 350 suicides have used it to speed nature's work. With its constant maintenance and repainting, plus the fact that it turns in a tidy profit as one of the most lucrative tourist attractions in history, the tower is now likely to stand just about indefinitely. Hardly anyone calls it ugly anymore. Indeed, with age, it grows more gracious, delicate and endearing.

The sprawling, majestic group of buildings known as the Hôtel des Invalides, near the Eiffel Tower, was Louis XIV's gesture to the thousands of soldiers who had been disabled in his interminable wars. Tucking away the wounded in their own palatial home—where they could enjoy free beds, meals, medical treatment, and tending their own individual vegetable gardens—salved the royal conscience. Better still, it got the war veterans off the Pont Neuf, where they had made a habit of begging rather too insistently. At one time there were as many as 7,000 mutilated men housed in Les Invalides but the handful that remain today from the last two World Wars make up little more than a guard of honour.

Les Invalides has become a museum famed for its perfect 17th-Century architecture, for its war relics ranging from spears to rocket launchers, for its paintings and murals, for its two churches, but most of all for the huge pit dug in the floor of the Église du Dôme: Napoleon's tomb. The wily little Corsican killed off the flower of French manhood by taking on most of the Continent—and England, too—in a series of imperial battles that bled France white and ended with total, final disaster at Waterloo. And yet, oddly enough, most of the French people maintain a perverse reverence for his memory. After all, his days of glory were more glorious than those of anyone else, including all the kings and Charles de Gaulle. There, in his final resting place under the dome, they have entombed him with fitting majesty and in full uniform. His bones are encased in six successive coffins: the first made of tin, the second of mahogany, the third and fourth of lead, the fifth of ebony and sixth of oak. His heart and stomach lie in sealed silver vessels between his legs, and holding the six coffins is a formidably thick and heavy sarcophagus of red porphyry brought from the wilds of the Russian province of Karelia.

There is a minority of Parisians, those who are not affected by *la Gloire*, who will tell you that the real reason for the sevenfold boxing job is to make sure that he never gets out again.

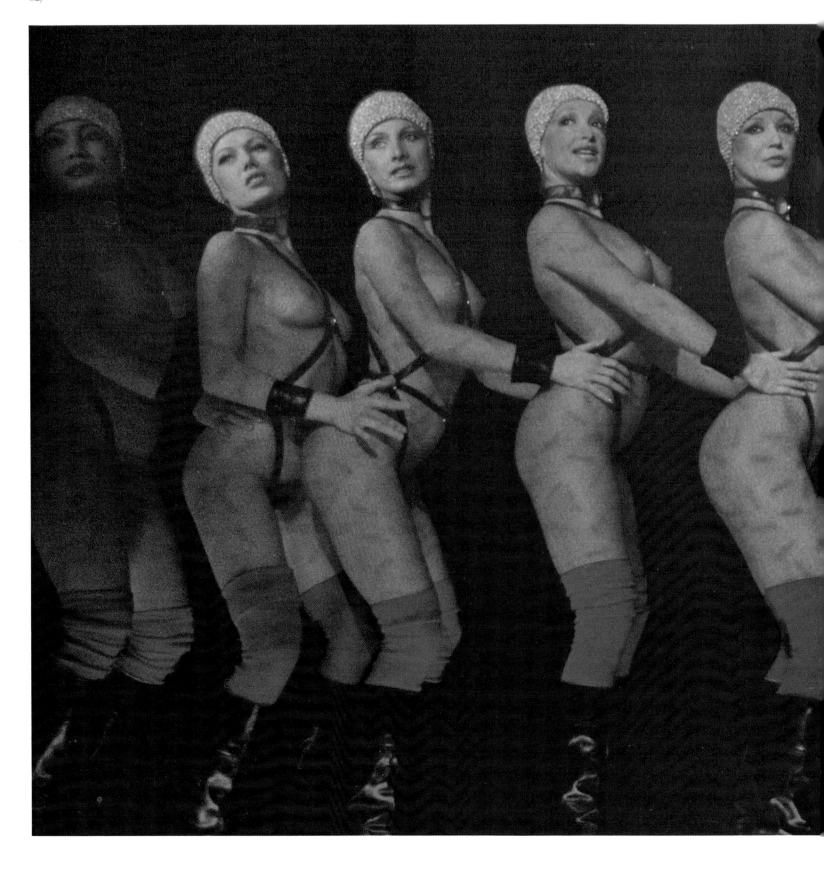

Crazy Nights at the Crazy Horse

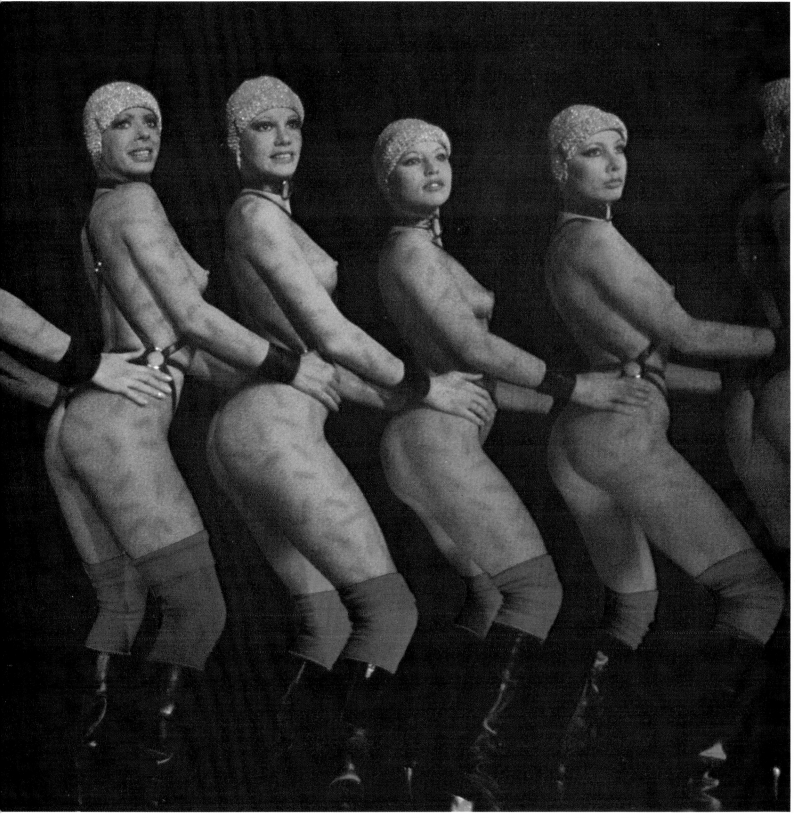

Spotlit to suggest pink bruises, dancers in boots and straps prance across the stage in a flaunting overture. "Le Crazy" is famous for inventive lighting.

Paris night life, world famous since the days of the can-can in the 19th Century, can still be sexy, witty and artistic. Shows at the Crazy Horse Saloon combine all three attributes exceptionally. Founded in 1951 by restaurateur Alain Bernardin, the Crazy Horse rapidly won a reputation for beautiful, undressed women and sophisticated dance routines. The high quality of the entertainment depends on Bernardin's rigid personal control. He drives his dancers hard in rehearsal and fires girls who allow their personal lives to prejudice their work. The 20 stunning girls employed there at any one time are given exotic stage names like Vanilla Banana and Greta Fahrenheit and they are always superb dancers. They have to be; the taut, original routines, which take weeks of practice to perfect, are in the most demanding tradition of modern dance.

A chequerboard of lights is used to accentuate a dancer's eyes and lips, which are, claims Crazy Horse proprietor Bernardin, woman's most alluring features.

In a number entitled "The Three Graces"—for the ancient goddesses of beauty—dancers assume an introverted, virginal pose reminiscent of a fragile tulipbud.

Dressed in ropes of pearls as she begins her avant-garde striptease routine, a Crazy Horse dancer named Polly Underground is poised like a startled animal.

With feline snarls and high kicks (top), the dancer sheds most of her pearls and struts through a finale wearing little more than the stripes of a spotlight.

Under cold, unglamorous rehearsal lights, the girls line up in tattered workaday tights and leotards to face the gruelling demands of learning a new routine.

4

Glory on the Right Bank

The French like to say you can tell that a man has reached middle age when he stops drinking Burgundy and switches to Bordeaux. The Bordeaux wines are generally more expensive, more delicate and full of nuance, thinner, *plus fin*; the Burgundies are full, rich, generous, redolent of youth and folly. It is a little bit the same with the two sides of the river in Paris. The Left Bank is Burgundy; the Right Bank, Bordeaux.

So it was that on a fine spring day in 1962 I found myself metaphorically aged long before my time, as I stalked warily across the river towards the enemy lines, over to the Right Bank and into that dimension commonly referred to as adulthood. I had a job as a foreign correspondent, working in offices just off the Champs-Élysées, *s'il vous plaît*. And as a member of that mystical coterie of high-powered international executives, intellectuals and Men of Destiny ($150 a week—wow! I had doubled my old newspaper salary), I would be able to savour the grown-up delights of credit cards, traffic jams and wash 'n' wear shirts, of inter-office memos, secretaries, conferences and long-distance 'phone calls. That was Right Bank stuff.

Since then things have become relative, as they always do. I found that my earlier Manicheism had been somewhat exaggerated. The Left Bank and Right Bank are not, after all, totally bi-polar: good-bad, black-white. Still, they *are* different, and the changes leap to the eyes the moment you get across the Seine. The Right Bank is the home of modern administration, with both the city hall (Hôtel de Ville) and the presidential residence (Élysée Palace); of most of the big department stores, the *grands magasins* (Les Galeries Lafayette, Le Printemps, La Samaritaine, La Belle Jardinière, Le Bazar de l'Hôtel-de-Ville); of the principal daily newspapers and international companies; of bank headquarters and large hotels; of the biggest parks and the most important railway stations; of fashion houses, expensive call girls and the vast majority of their clients.

No doubt about it: the Right Bank is grown-up. And, like grown-ups, it tends to take itself rather seriously. The French monarchs and republican heads of state have lived on the Île de la Cité (in the ancient Palais-Royal), near the present Place des Vosges (Hôtel des Tournelles), near the present Opéra (Palais-Royal), in the Louvre itself, in the Élysée Palace and, of course, in Versailles. But never, never, have they lived on the Left Bank of Paris. The Right Bank is not only grown-up, it is *sérieux*.

It is *sérieux* enough to be considered by the bureaucrats who decide such things as the centre of the city, the side on which the system of

Kicking footballs in what was once a royal park, children from near-by neighbourhoods use the Tuileries Gardens next to the Louvre as a playground. Before the formal gardens were created in the 16th Century, the site was occupied by a tile-making factory—a tuilerie—from which the gardens took their name.

arrondissements (literally, roundings out) begins. The *arrondissements*—the administrative districts into which Paris is divided—are laid out in a pinwheel pattern that starts at the heart of the Right Bank with the First Arrondissement, which includes the Louvre and the Palais-Royal. From there the numbering sequence spirals out in a clockwise direction, wheeling around and around until it finishes in the north-east—or upper-right-hand—corner of Paris with the 20th Arrondissement. The factory workers and artisans of the 20th Arrondissement are as *sérieux* as the businessmen of the First, or the furniture dealers of the 11th, or the princes, industrialists and *arrivistes* of the elegant 16th—indeed, as *sérieux* as the people of all the Rive Droite *arrondissements* in general.

They were from the very start. In the late 12th Century, when King Philippe-Auguste built the first defensive walls around his city, the people of the Right Bank were hard at work while the students across the Seine on the Left Bank were sitting with their masters in the meadows and vineyards of the Montagne-Ste-Geneviève. As so often happened in those days, the Church was the great pioneering influence, both physically and intellectually. Full of energy and conviction, monks went out into the Right Bank countryside, built their monasteries, and tilled the land and raised livestock to make themselves self-supporting. Just opposite the Île de la Cité is the oldest part of the Right Bank: the triangular area that even today is still called Le Marais, the Swamp. Monks were the first to settle there, digging and channelling and filling until they had drained the swamp dry and made it habitable for the secular settlers who soon swarmed over to it from the island. The monks had been preceded only by wandering tribesmen and soldiers; those who followed them—the farmers, workers and artisans who eventually became the bourgeoisie—were the true creators of Metropolitan Paris, a city that grew in a prolonged explosion, continually expanding beyond the medieval walls that were meant to delimit it.

From the start, what made Paris one of history's most successful urban developments, and what continues to do so today, was the peculiar mix of the bubbling human pot in which all levels and branches of society lived together—or, at least, side by side. No social separation—no workers' quarters at one side of the city and aristocrats' palaces at the other; from the earliest days of the Parisii the leaders and kings lived inside their city, surrounded by their irritable and difficult subjects, and in a permanent state of dialogue. When the king was a natural leader who knew how to maintain that dialogue—like our good *Vert-Galant*—he prospered with his subjects. When he refused the give-and-take of the dialogue, as did Louis XIV by moving 12 miles south-west to Versailles, or when he was inept at handling it, as was Louis XVI, trouble inevitably followed.

Today, still, the Marais is a good lesson in the unplanned urbanization that allowed Paris to prosper. It was there that the typical *hôtel à la française*

In this *vue à vol d'oiseau* (bird's-eye view) of 17th-Century Paris, the Louvre appears in the foreground in its original role as a huge formidable fortress located where the city wall met the Seine. Because the plan, drawn in 1615, looks to the east, the Right Bank is seen on the left and the Left Bank is seen on the right.

—the basic French design for a city mansion, with its beautiful stonework, staircases, high windows and wrought iron, built around a courtyard of geometrical gardens—began to evolve. The Palais Soubise, the Hôtel Carnavalet, the Hôtel de Lamoignon, the Hôtel d'Albret—all are stunning examples of this architecture; and—what is most important—they are not isolated, but planted in the midst of modest apartment buildings of the *petit peuple*. The privileged and wealthy of Paris have always had their grand *résidences*, it is true; but they have not been cut off from the stream of life in which the lesser populace swims.

The most striking example of unsuccessful urbanization that I know— what might be called "the anti-Paris"—is Leningrad. Like the Marais, Leningrad (originally St. Petersburg) was built upon a drained marsh; but it was planned from A to Z and never given the chance to grow organically. The result is a cold, inhuman disaster through which vast avenues (why city planners should find asphalt attractive I'll never understand) sweep with ineluctable majesty from one palace to another, from the River Neva to a statue, from a traffic circle to a park, and so on, making the whole confection as barren and humourless as an architect's model. Leningrad is a city made to amuse czars, to be displayed on picture postcards. The only thing the geniuses forgot when they planned it was the people.

In total contrast, the Marais teems with people and their creations; it is people-sized. The twisting little streets and alleys are an intricate web of stores and workshops and old apartment buildings and hotels that have hardly changed in the last 300 years. Even the names of the streets, especially the smaller ones behind the *hôtels à la française*, reflect labour: Rue du Grenier, Rue de la Verrerie, Rue de la Couture: Granary Street, Glassworks Street, Sewing Street. I have already mentioned an apparent contradiction: Place des Vosges, which is the focus of the Marais and its best symbol as well. It is undeniably beautiful, but it is also geometrical— as chilly, orderly and austere in aspect as Leningrad. The difference, though, is that it is a jewel planted in the rough setting of humanity, neither overpowering its neighbours nor being overpowered by them. They are mutually complementary. That is the secret of Paris.

King Philippe-Auguste (1165-1223) was the ablest European monarch of his time, the first son of France to prove himself a brilliant administrator, and the man who literally paved the way for Paris to become a great city, by commanding the first paving of its streets. He went on to embellish the city in many ways: building new churches (including work on Notre-Dame), new hospitals, the first new aqueducts since the Roman occupation and innumerable freshwater fountains. Most important of all, he surrounded the city with stout ramparts of awesome size—walls nine feet thick at the base, up to 30 feet high, dominated by 34 round towers on the Left Bank, 33 on the Right. The walls were breached by six fortified gates on either bank—each with its own design, its own name, its own legend. Within those walls Paris was able to build in safety for centuries.

In Philippe-Auguste's time Paris still lived in dread of attack and siege. The collective memory was graven with images of the bloodthirsty Norsemen who, again and again in the 9th Century, had rowed their longboats up the Seine and laid waste the city; and it was still accepted that only the divine intervention and uncanny powers of Geneviève had saved Paris from the rape of Attila the Hun. The need for a great defensive wall was obvious, but the task of encompassing a city that spanned both sides of the Seine set peculiar difficulties. When the wall was completed, therefore, one particularly vulnerable section remained: the south-western point, just below the Île de la Cité at the junction of wall and river. The king and his engineers recognized this natural weakness. What they needed was a fortress, and their solution was to build a ponderous dungeon, a southwestern stronghold that took the form of a tower 96 feet high and 144 feet in circumference, set in a great square of walls up to 13 feet thick. It was completed in the dawn of the 13th Century and called the Louvre.

From that time on, this amazingly protean edifice has been an integral part of the Paris scene. For Philippe-Auguste the building's justification was purely protective and functional, like an early version of a blockhouse. He stored in it his treasures, his archives and his arsenal, but never in the world did he think of living in it. Later—as new regimes came to power, as Paris grew outwards, as the Louvre actually became enclosed within the city—many monarchs did choose to live there. And while doing so, they added to it and decorated it until it became the vast, sprawling structure we see today, housing perhaps the greatest museum of art in the world. In fact, the huge building of today is a diminished Louvre: the western end, the Palais des Tuileries, was destroyed by fire in 1871, during the bloody days of the Paris Commune. But there was one unexpected and happy result of this destruction: the opening up of the long perspective that stretches from the little Arc de Triomphe du Carrousel, which before the fire had been hidden within the Louvre's courtyard, up to the immense Arc de Triomphe, the world-famous one at the top of the Champs-Élysées.

As Paris expanded, it tore down its old walls and turned the land they had occupied into streets. The city's second set of walls was put up by Charles V some 150 years after Philippe-Auguste. Charles decided that a strongpoint was needed at the eastern end of his expanded city, and for that purpose he built a tall, remarkably ugly, eight-towered bastion which he grandly named the Château Saint-Antoine but which the Parisians called "La Bastille" (the fortress). Over the centuries the Bastille became the most glaring symbol of authority and despotism—a place for locking up the Crown's opponents, but one never elegant enough to become, as the Louvre did, a royal residence. Even its construction was a nicely symbolic act of royal arbitrariness. The king's provost, Hugues Aubriot,

Exuding an unmistakable air of monied elegance that is characteristic of fashionable Paris society, a young bride sips a glass of champagne on the morning of her wedding day while one of Paris' chic coiffeurs dresses her hair.

laid the first ceremonial stone, then sent press gangs throughout the city to round up enough labourers to heave the prison's stones into position. But, according to legend, justice and irony were served: the Bastille's first prisoner was said to be Hugues Aubriot, arrested as a heretic after he had remonstrated against the odious new taxes introduced at the beginning of Charles VI's disastrous reign.

The taking of the Bastille by revolutionary mobs in 1789 has been described a million times, but most often too pridefully. In fact, it was surrendered but its garrison was nonetheless mercilessly butchered. Not a single trace of that fortress remains today because the revolutionary authorities sold it to a merchant of construction materials, a man named Palloy, who made an enormous profit by transforming stones and scraps of iron into "souvenirs of the Bastille"—stones carved to represent a relief plan of the fortress, leg-irons reforged into medals, dice-boxes, paper-weights, snuff-boxes and inkpots. Palloy even utilized paper documents left behind in the prison, having them made into playing cards or fans depicting scenes of the storming of the Bastille. Now, on that site, we have the large, circular Place de la Bastille and, in its centre, a tall black and green column—the Colonne de Juillet, commemorating those who died in July, 1830 in the "three glorious days" of revolution that put the bigoted Charles X to flight and cleared the way for a new constitutional monarch, Louis-Philippe, Duke of Orléans.

Incidentally, if Napoleon had had his way, they would have had to find somewhere else to put the July Column. The Emperor was very enthusiastic about erecting an 80-foot-high elephant on this spot to symbolize his intended conquest of the East. A full-scale model made of wood and plaster was put up initially in 1812; the plan was to make it a fountain with water gushing from the elephant's trunk. Then came Waterloo. For more than 30 years the model stood there moulding, an object of constant derision by Parisians; and when it was finally carted away, thousands of rats who had made it their home were turned out into the streets.

One of my favourite Right Bank structures very nearly met with the same fate as the Bastille. This is the Palais-Royal, the graceful, rectangular, arcaded building at the foot of Avenue de l'Opéra, opposite the Louvre. The revolutionaries had singled it out to be demolished for some hare-brained scheme, but happily the deputies regained their senses and voted to let it remain. Such cliff-hanging suspense was very much in character for this 17th-Century palace; there has probably been more intrigue, more pleasure-seeking, more trouble and more generalized hanky-panky in and around the Palais-Royal than in any other locality of Paris.

Oddly enough (or fittingly enough, anti-clerical cynics will say) the Palais-Royal began existence as the Palais-Cardinal, official residence of that most Gaullian of churchmen, Cardinal Richelieu. Lacking neither

Acknowledging the cheers of an enthusiastic audience (right), a puppeteer pops up with one of his stars to take a curtain call. At its permanent location just off the Champs-Élysées, this guignol (puppet show) has made itself a Right Bank tradition by playing for decades to successive generations of children.

intelligence nor ambition—nor influence over Louis XIII nor access to public funds—the cardinal built himself a sumptuous home worthy of his high opinion of himself, a residence considerably bigger and more lavish than the lodgings he had owned in the Place des Vosges. After all, one has to move up in life, doesn't one? When the cardinal went to his reward, he willed his house not to the Church but to the Crown, and so it became the Palais-Royal.

Louis XIV, as an active stripling, enjoyed his own share of debauch there, notably getting with child Louise de la Vallière, his favourite mistress. Jean-Baptiste Colbert, his great, all-purpose Minister, pushed State secrecy to extremes for the delivery: he brought in a doctor—who was blindfolded.

In 1780, when the palace fell into the hands of Louis-Philippe, Duke of Orléans, it became the most animated and elegantly sleazy location in town. This Louis-Philippe was a serious spender, if ever there was one, and chronically short of funds. Later known as Philippe-Égalité because of his bourgeois sympathies in the Revolution, he took the money-making expedient of remodelling the building into its present form, adding the arcaded pavilions that give on to three sides of the courtyard garden. He guessed that he would be able to sell the pavilion shops for a pretty penny, and he was right. He charged up to 50,000 *livres* per store—a very high price for the period—and the buyers swarmed in.

Down in Versailles, where the Revolution had not yet caught up with the Bourbons, Louis XVI poked fun at Louis-Philippe with the biting remark: "Cousin, now that you've set up shop I suppose we'll only be seeing you on Sundays." Philippe-Égalité got his revenge a few years later by voting with the revolutionaries in favour of separating Louis from his royal head. Then, in 1793, the wheel turned once again and he, too, was guillotined—one of thousands of victims of the Reign of Terror that indiscriminately eliminated royalists, aristocrats, priests and alleged traitors and counter-revolutionaries.

Regardless of political events, though, the garden and the pavilions of the Palais-Royal remained a den of mundane iniquity and pleasures of the flesh. Some of the best cafés and restaurants in Paris were located there, along with gambling dens, bordellos and even carnival-style galleries. Countless duels were fought there, crowds harangued, business and political deals and love affairs consummated. Late in the 18th Century one Parisian described it as "the meeting place of all the pimps, swindlers, pickpockets and rogues of the city". Among the carnival attractions there were a 19-year-old Prussian girl who stood seven feet tall and a man named Paul Butterbrodt (Bread-and-Butter) who was said to weigh more than 500 pounds. Perhaps it was all best symbolized by a little shack in front of which a notice advertised that for a small entry fee the stroller would be able to contemplate "what God himself may not even see". The money paid and shack entered, the eager curiosity-seeker found himself in front of a mirror, listening as a portentous voice intoned: "You now see your own likeness, which God can never do because there is nothing else like Him."

Although the Palais-Royal is quite cold and dignified today, and its shops eminently respectable and expensive, it is appalling to think that it might so easily have been obliterated by the destructive urge of those revolutionaries. And infinitely more horrific is the fact—not so well-known —that Notre-Dame de Paris was also marked out for the same fate as the Bastille. That ecclesiastical masterpiece escaped, providentially, only by Napoleon's accession to power. (The little Corsican was not a believer, but he needed the cathedral as a properly impressive setting for his coronation.) Before his accession, the dismantling of the cathedral, as a "quarry" for building stones, had been officially decided by the revolutionary hotheads. They were the same manner of men who, all over France, had pulled apart churches with teams of oxen and who, in the name of holy secularism, had sedulously placed ladders and scaffolds in front of cathedral portals to bash off the sculpted heads of the saints depicted there. Such Orwellian (I almost said Cromwellian) excesses are certainly not limited to France, but it is an unfortunate and undeniable fact that the French, like bright but unstable children, have a strong and wicked destructive instinct within them, one that they have turned most frequently upon themselves.

"I really do like the Parisians," a Canadian friend once protested to me. "But they are bloody-minded, aren't they?" How true. Much as I like and admire them, I have to admit that they can be absolutely impossible when they give way to those ancient tribal tugs of suspicion and self-indulgence, and allow their Latin tempers to overrule their God-given intelligence and *lycée*-imposed Cartesianism. This chronic irritability, as I have suggested earlier, doubtless springs from their native pride and the conviction that those above them are busy bending the rules on their personal behalf. At the same time, it must be said that the Parisians often lost their heads (metaphorically speaking) with very good cause. For example, it would have taken the serenity of a saint not to have been moved to churlishness by some of the excesses of the French throne. Louis XIV was by no means alone in taking extravagant self-indulgence to ridiculous extremes. A passion for ostentation (is there anything more absurd and affected than one of those golden Louis XV chairs that breaks when you sit on it?) has gripped so many French kings, princelings and political leaders that the domestic history of France could well be chronicled through the ever-more ingenious inventions by which finance ministers have squeezed money from the people to pay for high-level posturing.

"Paris is the one city in the world that has been the most destroyed over the ages," lamented French writer Georges Pillement, referring to the

/99

In an apartment that epitomizes Right Bank wealth and fine taste, an industrialist and his wife smile reservedly among his collection of art and French 18th-Century furniture, so magnificent that it has been given to the Louvre where space has been reserved to display it after the couple's lifetimes.

destruction wrought by its own citizens and kings so often scornful of ancient beauty in the face of opportunities for new construction. He left unspoken the irony that the city has been virtually untouched through the ravages of many French wars—since the departure of the Vikings, at any rate. However, when they weren't being squeezed too hard, and when times were propitious enough for them to indulge their natural talents for good living, the Parisians have rebuilt what they tore down. Often for the better—but not always.

As much as I find him preposterous and *antipathique*, I have to admit that Louis XIV, the Sun King himself, had an enormous and far-reaching effect on the development of Paris. He came up from Versailles only rarely (a banquet here, a ridiculous pageant there) but the vibrations of his style and taste reached deep into the heart of the city. It was Louis who ordered the building of the Royal Observatory and the royal tapestry factory of the Gobelins; it was Louis also who hired André le Nôtre, the greatest of French gardeners, to redesign the Tuileries Gardens west of the Louvre into the classically ordered form that we can still see today. With, in addition, Les Invalides, St-Sulpice, the octagonal Place Vendôme and the circular Place des Victoires (in which, guess who was the centrepiece subject? Louis himself, bigger-than-life, dominating the enchained "slave nations" of Spain, Holland, Prussia and Austria) Louis proved again and again his imperative need to impress upon the Parisians, those unworthy renegades, his fulsome magnificence.

Unlike *le Vert-Galant*, who built elegant residential quarters for citizens within the fabric of the city and who was concerned with giving them truly useful objects (the Pont-Neuf, as beautiful as it is utilitarian, was completed during his reign), the Sun King ordered up regal monuments. It was only incidental that people might be able to live in or near them. Today, Place des Victoires is only a ragged shadow of its former symmetry (originally all its buildings matched in style) but Place Vendôme is as stark, austere and wealth-reflecting as ever. No wonder the Hôtel Ritz is on one side, Van Cleef & Arpels on the other, and a host of banks, stockbrokers, insurance companies and diamond pedlars in between.

What Louis XIV started, his descendants—both by blood and power—continued with unfeigned delight. We owe the present Place de la Concorde to Louis XV who, in 1744 suffered a near-fatal illness. When he regained his health, a committee of Paris businessmen celebrated the event by commissioning a huge equestrian statue of the king, who was fondly known as *le Bien-Aimé*, the well-beloved. The king, in turn, graciously permitted his citizens to build a suitable setting for the statue: a grand square shaped as a raised octagon and surrounded by a dry moat 65 feet wide that was spanned by six stone bridges. In the centre was the statue of *le Bien-Aimé*, nobly astride a groaning horse, dressed like a Roman with the inevitable crown of laurels, and looking properly serene. It will perhaps come as no surprise that the name first given to the square was Place Louis XV. The irony, of course, is that *le Bien-Aimé's* grandson, Louis XVI, was beheaded there on January 21, 1793, by which time it was called Place de la Révolution. Two years later it became Place de la Concorde.

Long before that time, Louis XVI had proved luckless and feckless. In 1770, when he was the Dauphin and marrying Marie-Antoinette, the people were invited to this *place* for a royal fireworks display in his honour. Everything was planned to make a magnificent show, including grandstands for the people to sit in and fountains flowing with red wine for them to drink. Unfortunately, an ill-directed rocket fell upon a wooden shack where other fireworks were stored. The resulting fire caused a general panic and stampede in which 133 people died.

Whether it was horrible fact or only a wishful legend, it was said that when Louis XVI was tipped under the guillotine, the "national razor" on the first descent did its job only halfway. Accompanied by Louis' pitiful bellowing, it had to be raised again to make its way through the royal fat, sinew and bone.

"Ah, Liberty, what crimes are committed in thy name," cried the revolutionary, Madame Roland, before she died in her turn that same year of the Reign of Terror. In all, 1,119 victims of the Revolution ended their days on that same grisly scaffold, including Marie-Antoinette, Madame du Barry, Marat's assassin Charlotte Corday, and Robespierre and his friends, who had earlier dispatched so many others to their doom. At the height

Sun brings a warm blush to red-brick houses in Place des Vosges, Paris' oldest square. Built on the instruction of Henri IV, the square was completed in 1612.

of the executions, so folklore has it, a team of oxen pulling some freight refused to cross the *place* because of their instinctive fear of the smell of blood. For years afterwards debate raged as to whether death by the guillotine was instantaneous, and those arguing that it was not insisted most especially that Charlotte Corday blushed when a carpenter grabbed at her freshly severed head and struck it with his fist.

All of this grim detail tends to cloud the fact that the guillotine (or *la Louisette*, as it was also called) was conceived by a doctor of anatomy, one Joseph Ignace Guillotin, as a humanitarian gesture, to ensure a quick and painless end to the tribulations of those condemned to death. Before that, only nobility had been accorded the privilege of death by decapitation. Contrary to popular belief, Guillotin only *proposed* such an instrument. Its design was entrusted to Dr. Antoine Louis, an officer of the Academy of Surgery, and the first working model was built by Tobias Schmidt, a German harpsichord maker, who tested his machine on corpses at the Hôpital Bicêtre and on live sheep in the alley outside his shop. A highwayman called Pelletier was chosen as the first human "guinea pig"; he was executed in April, 1792, in Place de Grève in front of the Hôtel de Ville.

Today it is generally assumed that all of the Revolution's decapitations were staged at Place de la Concorde, but that is not so: 73 people were executed at Place de la Bastille and another 1,306 at Place de la Nation on the eastern edge of the city, making a grand total of 2,498. It is a fairly good score for political prisoners, but not a patch on a good war. And in case you were wondering: no, the ironies of history were not carried to their ultimate limit. Dr. Guillotin expired peacefully in bed in Paris in the year 1814, his head solidly attached to his shoulders. Until the end he complained bitterly because his name had been given to "Schmidt's machine".

For all the action Place de la Concorde has seen in the past (carnivals and fairs were occasionally set up there; and for years *desmoiselles* sold their favours on the grass of the dry moats, which since have been filled in), the place is rather a bore today—what one irreligious wit has called "the world's biggest traffic circle". Ironically, its pole of attraction that mysteriously sends hundreds of thousands of tourists scurrying at the peril of their lives through the murderous, high-speed flood of 20th-Century traffic is a 3,000-year-old obelisk—the oldest monument in Paris.

This 75-foot-high monolith, with its hieroglyphic ducks, owls and locusts glorifying Rameses II, was given to Charles X of France by the Viceroy of Egypt in 1829 and—like the later gift of Cleopatra's needle in London—ultimately set up, incongruously, in the middle of an alien city and an alien culture. It is like a curious bibelot on a living-room table, the souvenir of some distant voyage. But, in its favour, it does possess the single, overriding merit of not disturbing anyone. The simple truth (or, considering the people involved, the complicated truth) is that the Egyptian

A model gets a kiss from her couturier boss at a party on November 25 marking the annual festival of Ste-Catherine, by tradition the patron saint of young women working in the fashion industry. The extravagant hat reflects an old custom of garlanding Ste-Catherine's effigy on the saint's day. Women who are still unmarried at 25—referred to as 'Catherinettes' —mark the occasion by wearing hats such as this one to declare publicly their single status.

stone is there because no one could agree on the subject for a centrepiece that was purely French. The royalists naturally wanted Louis XVI, with a weeping willow (they didn't fear heavy-handed symbolism) planted next to him; the republicans wanted a huge flagpole, while some people favoured a fountain and others suggested Charlemagne. The obelisk, so nicely non-political, was a diplomatic compromise of which the French were excessively proud when, in 1836, military engineers unloaded it from a barge on the Seine and put it up without breaking it.

Place de la Concorde is handsome enough, but like so many national self-glorifications it smacks of the drafting table and mathematical planners. It affords plenty of spectacular views—the length of the Champs-Élysées, the Tuileries Gardens and across the Seine, the Eiffel Tower. But the only time it becomes truly beautiful in itself is when it can least be seen: at night, when the 600-odd lamps and spotlights throughout the *place* are thrown on and glow like a cloud of giant fireflies.

Lighting is very much a part of the ancient magic of Paris. "The City of Light" was a phrase I had heard for years; and for a long time I assumed that the romantic title was a metaphor referring to the spirit of the city, to the rationalism, the gaiety and the learning. But no: in history Paris was, quite literally, the "City of Lights". In the 14th and 15th Centuries it was as dark as a farmyard at night, with only three dim lanterns glowing (two at the entrances to fortified towers, one in a cemetery), but early in the 16th Century it rapidly changed when house-owners were constrained to put candles in their second-floor windows. Later, lamp-bearers were stationed at busy intersections, ready to lead anyone home with the aid of torches "metred" by hour-glasses.

Late in the 17th Century, the city distributed thousands of glass lanterns with candles inside, which were affixed to pulleys by upper windows. By the middle of the 18th Century the lanterns were replaced by the first *réver-bères*, metal oil lamps with a polished mirror placed behind the flame, causing it to throw all its light in one direction, to "reverse" the light. Never before then had a city been lit like Paris. It was like a Christmas tree, a breathtaking inspiration for foreign visitors.

In 1829 Paris became the first city in the world to be lit by gas lamps. With its *salons*, its cafés and restaurants, its opera, symphony and multitude of theatres, it glowed with a spiritual brilliance every bit as dazzling as its streets. The Revolution had run its bloody course. Napoleon I had come and gone. France had made an appalling sacrifice to indulge his military genius; nevertheless, the little "Corsican Adventurer" had proved a visionary administrator for Paris—commanding spectacular construction work on the Louvre, the laying out of the present Rue de Rivoli, the building of new bridges, squares, streets and markets, massive improvements in the city's water supply, its drains and quays. He had dreamed, so he said, of making Paris the true capital of Europe—"a city of two, three, even four million inhabitants, something fabulous, colossal. If I had only had twenty years and a little leisure, people would have looked in vain for Paris as it used to be."

Above all Napoleon left his mark on Paris in the shape of the largest triumphal arch in the world: 165 feet high, 148 feet wide, so spacious that an amateur pilot once flew a small aeroplane between its columns as a daredevil stunt. But Napoleon never lived to see the gigantic arch completed. When he finally passed beneath it, he was in a hearse on his long-delayed return from St. Helena.

Following his victories of 1805 Napoleon had ordered that they should be celebrated by the construction of two triumphal arches: the little Arc de Triomphe du Carrousel in the Tuileries and the Arc de Triomphe, supremely situated in the old Place de l'Étoile and crowning the majestic sweep of the Champs-Élysées. (Indeed, if he'd had his way, there would have been two more arches, one dedicated to Peace, one to Religion; but this plan, like his earlier scheme for the Bastille elephant, never materialized.) Today the Étoile (star) seems such an obvious location for his greatest monument, standing as it does at the hub of 12 avenues radiating star-wise. But it was far from obvious in 1806 when building began. The

While an employee works behind the scenes at the Espace Cardin preparing the next lot of art for auction, an auctioneer in the brightly lit sales room invites bids for a painting that his assistant holds aloft. This gallery and many of Paris' other dealers in fine art and valuable antiques are located on the Right Bank.

Étoile was then situated on the outskirts of the city—on a reclaimed rubbish dump. And the ground was so chalky and unstable that construction costs soared and soared, ultimately topping ten million francs.

When, after 30 years of much-interrupted work, the arch was finally finished, only a handful of people turned out in torrential rain to see its inauguration. Today, at least half a million visit it every year. Much more than a monument to Napoleon's revolutionary armies, it is now France's pre-eminent national shrine; the Tomb of an Unknown Soldier, set in the ground beneath the arch, was dedicated on November 11, 1923. Every evening the eternal flame marking the tomb is symbolically revived by a party of ex-servicemen, who parade before it.

Officially, the Arc de Triomphe no longer stands in Place de l'Étoile, but in Place Charles de Gaulle. In 1970, by a slender majority and amid bitter public protests, the Council of Paris voted to change the name of the celebrated hub of the city. But stubbornly, a great many Parisians will always continue to use the old name of Étoile that is so firmly rooted in the national heritage.

Respecting a monarch has never come naturally to the citizen of Paris. Life is too short for awe; he would rather complain about a king's wicked strumpet of a wife or draw cartoons of Charles de Gaulle with a nose a foot long. In this way, de Gaulle's years of power struck me as extremely dangerous for the well-being of the Parisian soul: for too many people were speaking as if they actually respected him. De Gaulle, for his part, had few illusions about his subjects. His most penetrating analysis of France came in the form of a question: how can you govern a country with 400 varieties of cheese?

Of all French rulers, it was Napoleon III who most deeply marked Paris. It was he, in fact, who gave us most of the Paris of today. Carried to imperial power by the typically Bonapartian expedient of a *coup d'état* in 1851, Napoleon III was bursting with as many grand designs as he was with pretensions; and, like the first Emperor of the French, one of the corner-stones of his ambitions was the remaking of Paris—sweet, easy living Paris—into a modern city that the whole world might envy. Debate still rages as to whether he should be thanked or execrated for his determination in that direction, but he had it and he carried it through—with the help of a wilful, thick-skinned and yet admirable man named Baron Georges-Eugène Haussmann.

The man Napoleon III chose as his instrument was a civil servant, known for his efficiency and bulldozer ruthlessness in carrying out superior orders. Napoleon III made Baron Haussmann prefect (chief executive) of the Department of the Seine, unrolled his maps and told him to reshape the city. Haussmann did—and with a vengeance. During the 17 years of his tenure (1853-1870) he turned Paris into a workyard—brazenly evicting the population, ripping down buildings and laying out wide, new streets and avenues where only medieval tracks had existed before. He gave the city its present system of *grands boulevards*, tree-lined and faced with the six, seven, and eight-storey *résidences bourgeoises* that still stand today. Via aqueducts he brought drinking water to the city from as far as a hundred miles away, dug the cavernous underground canals of the sewer system which is so extraordinary that tourists still suffer the smell to take guided boat trips on it, modernized the city's lighting. In short, he prepared Paris for the big-time capitalism of the 20th Century.

Although Haussmann certainly did his work on the "student" side of the river (Boulevard St-Germain, Boulevard St-Michel, Rue des Écoles, Rue de Rennes) the nature of his grand design was essentially upper-middle class and business oriented: quintessentially Right Bank. Indeed, one might say that he transformed the right bank into the Right Bank.

Even before Haussmann's time the few boulevards had been places of relaxation. Now they were filled with the music of Offenbach and, a little later, of the Moulin Rouge, the "naughty" French can-can, the naughtier novels and plays, and the posters of Toulouse-Lautrec. Now Paris was the centre of wit, education and style, just as it had been the centre of learning and majesty; and that style is still there today. Whatever sparks may fly in other cities of the world, Paris remains *the* great centre of fashion. But then, again, it always was; as far back as the 13th Century, contemporary accounts describe tailors "who were overwhelmed by their tasks, working night and day for gentlemen and great persons, and who are so skilful that they can deliver the next morning a robe ordered in the evening".

Haussmann shook Paris, pulled it apart and put it back together again, in the image of the bourgeois emperor he was serving. So thoroughly did he change the city that an estimated 60 per cent of Paris' present buildings date from the 17 years of his tenure. Moreover, the fact that he could effect all the changes relying only on horses and oxen and picks and shovels—virtually no construction machinery had yet been invented—testifies to the incredible energy the French can emit when they finally agree to something—or, as so often happens, when they are forced to agree to something.

Much of this work was accomplished by borrowing funds without being too careful about obtaining legislative sanction (some wag who knew his Offenbach dubbed the story of his dealings, "The Tales of Haussmann") and the ensuing *scandale* eventually drove Haussmann from office, although not before he had completed the major part of his plans. The criticisms levelled against Haussmann went far beyond the ethics of financing. His detractors argued that he had ripped up beautiful old districts that contained thousands of worthy artistic and architectural creations and that, worst of all, he had even dared to lay low Paris' most sacred living museum: the Île de la Cité. The entire space around Notre-Dame had been a wonderland of medieval vestiges—including the house where Abélard first put his scholarly hands on the fair Héloïse—of a value only slightly less than the cathedral itself. Yet Haussmann wiped them out with the self-assurance and bull-headedness of an emperor and replaced them with the most mediocre and undistinguished of buildings. As a result only in towns like Rouen, Strasbourg or Le Mans may we now have the privilege of viewing French cathedrals in their proper settings. What a terrible pity it is that people with enterprise, ambition and power rarely have a sense of humanity and aesthetics as well.

But Haussmann was, at least, practical; no doubt about that. There were sound strategic reasons for clearing away the medieval rabbit warrens in favour of broad, straight avenues. An insurrection in the maze of ancient streets and alleys, complete with easily defended barricades, was a very real and pressing nightmare to the administration. Both Napoleon III and his uncle Napoleon I, had ridden to power on the heels of revolutions; both in turn, felt the dangerously shifting sands beneath their feet. In the views of Haussmann and his emperor, Boulevard des Capucines and Avenue de l'Opéra and Rue des Écoles and, yes, even the magnificent Champs-Élysées, with that extravagant *arc de triomphe* crowning it, were military roads, down which troops could march abreast, enjoy a clear field of fire and easily sweep away any incipient barricades.

So, Haussmann was a rascal. But he did modernize Paris; and Paris had to be modernized, especially its water, lighting and sewage systems, all of them still marvellously efficient. In the man's favour, it must also be said that he gave Paris the great parks of the Right Bank. Everyone knows the Bois de Boulogne, a near wilderness when Napoleon III gave it to the city and now a 2,113-acre wonderland that is the indispensable lung of Paris. But just as important to the poorer folk who cannot afford to live in such a chic quarter are the parks at Buttes-Chaumont in the north-east, Vincennes in the east and Montsouris in the south. Paris shall have greenery, Napoleon III had decided after his long periods of exile in London, and he was as good as his word. The parks he established are as beautiful as ever. The boulevards, alas, are now mere funnels for automobiles and one of Haussmann's greatest creations has disappeared entirely: Les Halles.

Les Halles, or "the belly of Paris", as Zola called the food halls, were the last word in modern urban planning when they opened in the 1860s. The city's central market had been there—opposite the Île de la Cité, north-east of the Louvre—since the 12th Century. If ever there was a colourful, popular, rough-and-tumble place in the city, this was it. Merchants and hustlers of all kinds came together with their wares and scales, surrounded by normally attendant fauna: cooks and servants and wenches buying their masters' provisions, pickpockets and knaves earnestly endeavouring to reach them before all their *sous* were gone, jugglers and clowns, whores and soldiers and promenaders. For centuries, too, amusement and edification had been provided here by the municipal pillory, an octagonal stone tower with a one-room apartment for the king's hangman at ground level and a big, horizontal wheel on the flat roof. Miscreants were held fast in the rim of the wheel, through which adjustable openings had been artfully pierced for heads and wrists. The wheel had a capacity of up to six persons, and the hangman (his duties also encompassed these lesser punishments) gave it a quarter-turn every 15 minutes, while honest folk tarried to watch the spectacle. Where possible, the punishment fitted the crime: sellers of rancid butter paraded with their wares plastered on their heads and waterers of milk were obliged to drink far more than their fill of their own mixtures. As for purveyors of rotten eggs, the ordinance read: "Every man who will have sold rotten or spoiled eggs shall be exposed on our pillory; the said eggs shall be abandoned to children who in manner of farce and joy, shall disport themselves by throwing them at his face to make everyone laugh." It was a jolly place that Haussmann chose to modernize.

For this challenge he turned to the famous architect Victor Baltard, who, after one false start in massive stone, found a perfectly Parisian solution by using the shockingly new materials of wrought iron and glass to create handsome, umbrella-like buildings. The design was ideally light and elegant and logical; and those buildings, eventually models for city markets the world over, will always be the sentimental favourite of everyone who knew Paris before 1970.

Iron pillars line an aisle in Notre-Dame du Travail.

Adventures in Metal

Visionary 19th-Century French architects eagerly embraced iron as a new building material. Some of their works, such as the Eiffel Tower and Les Halles marketplace (now-vanished), earned particular fame. Others, like those pictured here, are less well known but of great interest to architectural historians. In 1868, when Henri Labrouste designed the Bibliothèque Nationale's reading room (right), he was able to flood the hall with plenty of natural light by supporting the glass-domed roof on only 16 slender, metal pillars. And in 1901 Jules Astruc defied the stone-and-brick tradition of religious architecture by using naked iron in a church: Notre-Dame du Travail (above).

Readers in this huge room of the Bibliothèque Nationale see by light pouring through nine glass domes supported on elegant iron columns 30 feet high.

In the first chapter, I referred to my love for markets. Well, Les Halles was the ultimate market. Although restricted in theory to wholesalers, it was always too big (more than 20 acres), too open and too wonderful to be limited to mere stock-shuffling. Under the 12 soaring pavilions, and on the streets and sidewalks all around them, there arrived pre-dawn each day everything edible from every corner of France, delivered by every means of transportation and displayed for the buyers' inspection. It was more than a display, though; it was a veritable orgy, a mountain, a Niagara of food. What human being, even one light of stomach, would not be stricken with awe and lust by walking through a canyon of raspberries, a scented alley of mint, thyme and tomatoes? By the mid-1960s the Baltard pavilions were surfeited and the show of food spread outwards as far as Rue de Rivoli and as far east as Boulevard de Sébastopol. But that made the scene even more appealing. Crates of vegetables and fruits were miraculously stacked six, 10, 12 feet high, and late-night revellers made their way through the labyrinth like rats lost in a cheese factory, dodging the delivery men who charged recklessly ahead at the wheels of their little flat-backed stock-trucks, holding down their beep-beep horns and somehow avoiding homicide as they went about their duties, as full of *vin blanc sec* as the tourists were of astonishment.

For your information that is a good point to remember: when you come to France, as you surely will, drink only white wine if you have work to do. It revivifies, whereas red wine tends to induce sleep. At least that is the folk tradition. After returning from a nocturnal visit to Les Halles (the great pleasure in those days was to continue a good evening with a ramble in the company of friends through the strawberries and then into a bowl of onion soup at one of the innumerable bistros) a very wise and irreproachably rectitudinous colleague of mine once made the telling observation: "You know, I've just about never seen a Frenchman really drunk. But then again, I've just about never seen one really sober, either."

They took down Les Halles in 1971, and, as much as I loved it, I can appreciate that it really had to go. Considering the titanic traffic jams caused by the huge, articulated lorries that rumbled in from all parts of the country and parked together every night in the heart of the city, considering the insalubrity and rat-infestations, considering all the complicated imperatives of modern commerce, it was inevitable that the wholesale market would have to be rationalized. In the case of Paris, they did it by moving the entire operation (yes, including the all-night restaurants, the all-night girls and even, some say, the rats) to modern and rather sterile quarters in the south, near Orly Airport, where the stalls can be efficiently reached by air, rail and super-highways.

The pavilions are gone now, and it is a very great pity because they were so handsome to look at and a natural centre of street life and spontaneous animation. The well-ordered municipal service complex that has replaced them is obviously more fitting to 20th-Century needs; all the same, I shall always feel a special nostalgia for that incredible pageant of Les Halles. Above all, I shall fondly remember the day I became a buyer there.

It happened when three Russian friends of mine came to town. We had spent a long evening together, punctuated by the innumerable toasts that are medicinally customary in chilly Muscovy, where, as everyone knows, polar bears amble down the streets and people have icicles hanging from the ends of their noses. By the end of our wassailing my Bolshevik pals had managed to reduce considerably the size of their icicles, but the resultant thaw had left them with a strange and unquenchable passion: they wanted to eat some apples. Now, apples are not exactly unknown in Muscovy, but compared with the variety and quality to be found in Paris, the Red varieties are mouthfuls of ash and gall. So, being the appointed Santa Claus in this glittering paradise where everything was available, I naturally took it upon myself to lead them forthwith to Les Halles.

Shortly before dawn we arrived to find the market a chaos of light and noise and activity, perhaps made all the more brilliant by our spirited state. Leading an uneasy path through the labyrinths, I managed at length to locate Apple Paradise, where Goldens and Granny Smiths and Reinettes and Richareds and Calvilles lay in absurd profusion, shepherded by a large, rubicund woman in a black apron who looked as though she had grown them all herself and could break your arm at the slightest misdirected word. Throwing caution—and my American accent—to the winds, I brazenly told her that as a restaurateur I qualified as a customer and would she sell me some of her wares, please, thank you very much.

Cocking an eye that had not been duped by anything or anyone, least of all a man, in the last 30-odd years, she replied: "Restaurant, huh? Which one?" "Chez Vladimir," I blurted, grasping at the first straw that entered my Soviet-saturated mind.

She nodded, shrugged and jerked her thumb over at the Goldens. "The minimum's one case."

I paid, took her receipt and then, seizing the crate of fruit, hurried back to where my three proletarians were waiting, their eyes glistening. Whenever I visit Moscow, my friends still talk of making another trip to Paris. I haven't dared tell them about what has happened to Les Halles.

Exuberant Flourishes of Fantasy

The riotous tracery of this verandah railing, designed in typical Art Nouveau fashion by Hector Guimard, stretches wrought-iron to its most expressive level.

Paris is a city to be looked at—a mélange of architectural styles. Among the most eye-catching are Art Nouveau buildings, reflecting the movement that sprang up in the 1890s as a flamboyant challenge to the heavy, sterile classicism of the time. Art Nouveau produced structures characterized by decorative lines that coiled like tendrils and unfolded like new leaves. Inspired in part by sinuous Japanese art and the natural, swirling shapes of the plant world, Art Nouveau rapidly found brilliant exponents. The florid stone and wrought-iron works of Hector Guimard, Jules Lavirotte and Louis Louvet embodied the ideals of the style, which fused romance with functionalism. By 1914 the lyrical extravagance of Art Nouveau had lost its appeal, but it left Paris many mementoes of its brief flowering that are still admired today.

Like a living plant the stonework curls about the doorway, then climbs to embrace a window above.

An Explosion of Vitality

Façades gave Art Nouveau designers a chance to dramatize their febrile visions.
This kind of architectural adornment reached a peak with Jules Lavirotte, whose
doorway for a 1900 house (above and right) today draws students of the style from
all over the world to its Avenue Rapp location. Lavirotte imbued his design with
so much energy and fluidity that he seems almost to have brought the stone to life.

A young woman's stone hair undulates sensually, as if ruffled by a breeze.

A gamine, hand placed provocatively on stone hip, gazes down from her aerie.

A bizarre hybrid of animal and plant decorates a panel of the glazed door.

The serpentine twists of an ornamental lizard let it double as a door handle.

Slim metal stalks support bud-shaped electric lights on a Métro stairway.

Shelters for the Métro

The most distinctive and widely visible reminders of the age of Art Nouveau are the many surviving Métro station entrances designed by Hector Guimard in 1900 for the Paris Métro Company. These metal structures so typified the curled, vegetal and delicately skeletal qualities of Art Nouveau that the whole movement was popularly known as "Style Métro".

Suggesting a fan of delicate petals, this elegant Art Nouveau canopy of frosted glass strengthened by ribs of metal shelters the entrance of a Métro station.

The handrail zigzags downwards like a toboggan run.

After snaking up three storeys, a section of the staircase uncoils itself above a display gallery.

A Swirling Sweep of Stairs

The long, influential tendrils of Art Nouveau
made their way into the Grand Palais,
Paris' big exhibition hall. This wide staircase,
with flowing, elegant wrought-iron railing
designed by Louis Louvet, exemplifies
the vital, romantic spirit of the style.

The staircase balustrades, with their writhing, whiplash design, enclose a broad sweep of steps intended to cope with crowds visiting the Exposition of 1900.

5

Forgotten Corners of the City

On the back terrace of a reconditioned farmhouse near Chartres some years ago I heard the most vivid and loving recollection of Paris—and of a particular Paris neighbourhood then unknown to me—I had ever encountered. It was all the more striking because the woman talking to me was describing, from first-hand experience, a period long since past. The woman's name was Simone Berteaut, and I had gone out to the country to interview her about the 30 years she had spent with her celebrated half-sister, Edith Piaf.

She was a curious little woman, La Berteaut: tiny (only five feet tall and weighing 85 pounds), with a funny, crooked gaze and a manner of speaking that was vulgar yet endearing and full of unexpected interjections. To add to the curious effect, she had a pet monkey riding on her shoulder or hopping about hysterically in her arms, a young man playing the role of houseboy-companion, and a roving hand that in a trice picked up and emptied her guests' wine glasses into her own as soon as the young man's back was turned.

We talked about Edith Piaf that whole afternoon, but the singer and Paris were so inextricably intertwined in Berteaut's reminiscences that the two came together like some trick film image. Inevitably so—because Piaf took Paris as the symbol of her whole being, and Paris found a human embodiment in Piaf. Never before had an artist so completely identified with a city; and never—even when she was singing the songs of professional hacks—had one artist been able to express so movingly the sentiment buried under the carapace built up over the centuries around the Parisian soul.

Piaf *was* Gavroche, Victor Hugo's child of the streets. She came from a background so poor that she was literally born on a pavement of Paris, under a *réverbère* street lamp on a policeman's outspread cape. Her parents—a fairground singer and a wandering acrobat—never had the means to feed her properly; for several years, as a little girl, she lived as a sort of mascot or good-luck charm in a provincial bordello where she was provided with enough nourishment for the body and plenty of human warmth for the soul. More or less abandoned by her parents, uneducated and hungry, she took to begging and singing in the streets as naturally as instinct tells animals to survive. She had a beret, a black sweater and a black skirt and, sometimes, shoes. The beret was for collecting coins. When Simone Berteaut, 13, joined the act, Piaf was 16 and already a seasoned professional entertainer.

In her charcuterie—a delicatessen and pork speciality shop—in the outlying district of Levallois, a woman leans over a display of pâté and sausage to clean the window. In the backwaters of Paris, many shops still maintain the décor and atmosphere of a bygone era.

Piaf's Paris was the eastern region of Belleville and Ménilmontant, still the city's poorest quarters. "Ah, Ménilmontant!" Berteaut sighed nostalgically. "Go look at Cité du Labyrinthe next time you're in the area. Then you'll understand what it was like for us. That was really where we started." And of course I went up there the very next day. How could I not pay a visit to a place with a name like that, and at the personal recommendation of Piaf's sister? Standing on those gritty old cobblestones, gazing up at the crowd of drab old workshops and apartment buildings that leaned against each other for support, I think I did understand what it must have been like for them. Paris doesn't have any true slums in the English or North American sense of the word; and this was the closest thing to them I had seen in the city.

Here, little Edith and Simone had planted their ill-shod feet and bony legs on the same cobblestones, turned their faces upwards and, by God, extracted *money* from the pinched, impoverished faces in those buildings. Here, Piaf had developed the incredible voice that rose like an extra-human force from her bird-like frame; and here in Cité du Labyrinthe, along Rue des Cascades, in Passage des Soupirs, on all the indifferent working-class streets, she had learned to express the yearning and the sadness that moved poor people to crack open their change purses and throw a *sou* or two down at the pair of urchins below them.

The same unmistakable sincerity remained in the later years of her success, and it was still powerful enough to make the same people—and then the bourgeois and the intellectuals, too—buy her recordings in vast quantities and fill the halls to bursting whenever she made a personal appearance. The voice took her from Belleville and Ménilmontant to the Champs-Élysées and the 16th Arrondissement, but until her death in 1963 Piaf always remained essentially a child of Cité du Labyrinthe.

"*Les gens du pavé, c'est différent des gens du trottoir,*" Berteaut told me that afternoon near Chartres. "People of the paving stones aren't the same as sidewalk people." And how thoroughly the two girls were marked by the *pavé* was comically demonstrated in the times of glory and success, when Piaf bought a *hôtel particulier* (a mansion) in the chic suburb of Boulogne—and then lived with Simone in its *concierge's loge.* "The joint had a great marble bathroom," Berteaut recalled for me. "Gold fixtures and all the rest. But we kept goldfish in the tub. You see, Edith never did like to wash. She had dirty feet all her life."

Les gens du pavé are still there around the Belleville area, but they are no longer quite the same. They have changed with the district itself. The hill—Belleville stands on a *butte* that is second in height only to Montmartre—has been transformed by bulldozer and crane into a typical, and not particularly distinguished, example of modern urbanization, with high, widely-spaced towers standing along the ridge. The people in the new

Joined by a couple of clowning males, two solidly built dancers of the rowdy can-can kick up their heels in this 1880s photograph, taken at the Moulin Rouge, the best known Paris dancehall of the era. The girl on the left is "La Goulue", whose uninhibited performances made her a popular sensation.

lodgings enjoy far better living conditions of course. In Piaf's youth, those picturesque old buildings had neither hot water nor anything better than communal toilets—one ancient, airless *cabinet d'aisances* at each turning of the steps between landings. And their inhabitants were cramped, cold in winter, and often exploited by ruthless absentee landlords.

It wasn't funny, a life with dirty feet; but there was also a certain charm and, yes, even a kind of grace about such a neighbourhood, as there is about all the other villages of Paris—a quality of life now disappearing. As people lock themselves inside their faceless skyscrapers and watch television, as life becomes inner-directed, standardized, egotistical, the spectacle is on the small screen, no longer on the broad sweep of the street. In most cities today it would appear that raising the standard of living across the board automatically creates an anti-human environment. That is why I always find myself drawn back to less well-known corners of Paris where something of the spirit of Piaf's Ménilmontant and Belleville survives, to long rambles through islands in the city that have been so far left completely untouched.

"*Ménilmontant, mais oui madame, c'est là, que j'ai laissé mon coeur,*" sang Charles Trenet, a contemporary of Piaf and second only to her in his rapport with the French soul. He was saying, of course, that he left his heart in Ménilmontant; and as sappy as that sounds, it was—like most clichés—probably a little bit true. It is—or was—that sort of a place.

Working-class Ménilmontant and industrial Belleville scarcely figure on the tourists' map of Paris; indeed, guide-books tend to dismiss the eastern districts in general as holding little appeal for the visitor. Yet, it is eastwards —decidedly, most things strange and odd and wonderful seem to lie in the mysterious East—that we find many of the more off-beat curiosities and surprises of Paris, including most notably that glorious eccentricity called Père Lachaise Cemetery. There, fittingly, Piaf found a resting-place right in the heart of her own Ménilmontant.

Named for a lascivious and luxury-loving Jesuit priest who was father confessor to Louis XIV, Père Lachaise is Paris' biggest and most fashionable cemetery, and easily its most interesting as well. Its 106 acres at any one time are home to probably more birds per square inch than any other spot in Paris, including the Bois de Boulogne; plus 300 to 400 stray cats who have become permanent residents, an uncounted number of dogs and other critters, and the most fabulous collection of necromantic statuary this side of the Pyramids. But whereas Cheops and other Pharaohs produced their creations with gigantic and impressive simplicity, the Parisians have expressed themselves freestyle in Père Lachaise, and in Baroque profusion.

The hills and dales of Père Lachaise, in themselves first-rate examples of the art of landscaping, teem with such an array of stone, steel and concrete memorabilia that a serious visitor with a feeling for history could easily spend a week there without exhausting his curiosity. There are life-size representations, larger than life-size representations, at least one full-scale ballerina in a tutu, animal statues of all sorts ranging from boxer dogs to pelicans, inventions proudly brandished in stone hands, every imaginable manner of angel and cherub and, not incidentally, whole chorus lines of clothed, half-clothed and naked nymphs in the most equivocal poses.

An air of distinguished eroticism seems to pervade the place, in memory of the father confessor himself; and the byways, alleys, nooks and crannies provide ideal trysting places for lovers and no less ideal viewing posts for the clans of voyeurs who make the cemetery the prowling ground of their predilection. Some of the earliest star boarders at Père Lachaise were Molière, La Fontaine and (top-of-the-bill in the 19th Century) Héloïse and Abélard, whose tombs are much less frequently visited today than those of Isadora Duncan, Chopin, Colette, Modigliani, Proust, Rossini, Bizet, Sarah Bernhardt and, most popular of all, Piaf. Everyone knows, too, that Oscar Wilde reposes in Père Lachaise beneath an Epstein carving, but not many are privy to the awful secret of his mutilation, as recounted by Michel Dansel in his sly little book, *Au Père Lachaise*: "The writer is represented in stone in the form of a winged sphinx. His statue was the victim of an injurious mutilation: two English women, who were promenading in Père Lachaise, were unable to suppress their indignation when they saw Oscar Wilde represented with such assuredly honourable virile attributes. They

Bursting with ribald glee, two comic artistes— one a midget—present an appallingly sugary parody of a classical ballet at a Right Bank nightclub, the Ange Bleu. Paris' legendary night life offers everything from the most intimate to the most lavish acts, including fashionable, if somewhat grotesque, shows like this.

seized stones from the edge of the alley and broke off his testicles. Cemetery guards carried these precious pieces to the main office, where for two years they served as paperweights for the conservator."

Not far from Père Lachaise, in the little-frequented eastern corner of Paris near Bois de Vincennes, there is another cemetery that provides an odd footnote to history: it was the only spot in France where the American flag flew throughout the Second World War, even during the Nazi occupation. The Cimetière de Picpus is a tiny private graveyard reserved exclusively for descendants of nobles who, during the Revolution were decapitated at the Place de la Nation (then known as Place du Trône Renversé: Overthrown Throne Square). Lafayette, the hero of the American Revolution, married into a *décapitée* family and thus earned his place in Picpus. The Stars and Stripes have flown over his tomb ever since his inhumation in 1834. During the Second World War the Germans respected the tradition and permitted Old Glory to stand untouched. The gesture was generous enough, but perhaps it was best explained by the fact that a high wall around the cemetery blocked the sight of the flag from all but passing aircraft.

Of all the villages that Paris absorbed as it expanded over the centuries, there are still a few that have managed to maintain a separate identity, a character that is somehow different from the bulk of the city surrounding them. The first example that springs to mind is, of course, Montmartre, due north of the Île de la Cité and, at 423 feet, the high point of Paris. Montmartre was not incorporated into Paris until 1860, and thus Baron Haussmann—who remade Paris through his grand architectural schemes —never got around to laying his hands on it. As a result it remains strikingly provincial, a gem of a little town situated on a hill, now hemmed in by the city and yet undisturbed by the activity that swirls around it at the foot of the *butte*. And although it can hardly qualify as "unknown Paris", it still has its quiet, unpolluted backwaters.

There was always something special about the heights of Montmartre, more so than, say, Belleville, whose high point is only six-and-a-half feet less. Early Celtic tribesmen worshipped their gods there, and so did the Romans. The very name of the hill is of religious origin, probably being derived from Mons Martis or Mons Mercurii (the Roman gods Mars and Mercury), or possibly from Mons Martyrum because St-Denis—the city's first bishop—was decapitated there in the 3rd Century A.D., before all the citizens of Paris had become quite convinced of the benefits of Christianity.

Ecclesiastic legend has it that Denis superbly one-upped the disbelievers by stooping down and picking up his own white-bearded head (halo attached, by the way), washing it off in the fountain of Rue de l'Abreuvoir and walking six thousand paces due north into the plain—a long enough stroll for any 90-year-old man, but downright miraculous for one with a

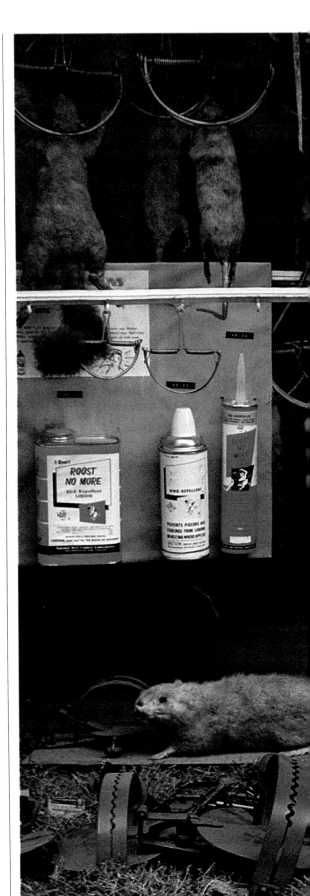

Stuffed rats and a stuffed fox demonstrate the efficacy of a wide range of lethal-looking traps sold by a pest-control shop in old Les Halles district.

severed head. Denis finally surrendered his head to a pious old lady named Catulla and expired. On that spot the Basilica of St-Denis was built, as the first example ever of that great Parisian invention, Gothic architecture. Here, in subsequent years, French kings were traditionally laid to rest.

At least two convents were built on Montmartre in the early days, as well as numerous churches. Squeeze a church in France, they say, and you generally get wine. This certainly applied to Montmartre. The vineyards of Clos de Montmartre produced a red nectar that was probably as tart as it was low in alcohol (much too far north for superior quality), but the wine was a great favourite of local philosophers and artists, most notably Jean-Jacques Rousseau. Quite possibly, Rousseau was impressed by its medicinal reputation, immortalized in the Parisian dictum: "He who drinks a pint of Montmartre wine pisses out four."

Curiously enough, there is still a small vineyard on the slopes of Montmartre. It occupies a fenced-in half-acre of precious, undeveloped land at the corner of Rue des Saules and Rue St-Vincent, in the shadow of the huge, alabaster-white Sacré Coeur Basilica. There are 1,800 vines in the vineyard, samples from all around the world, mixed in defiance of all good sense and good taste into a yearly harvest that yields just 500 bottles of a weird, hybrid wine of no distinction whatever but very high price. The name, *Clos de Montmartre*, is so prestigious, however, that notables and restaurateurs from every corner of the globe flock to Paris every May for the auction of the wine.

That unfortunately is a rather accurate reflection of what Montmartre has now become. It had to happen that the great resident artists—men like Berlioz, Nerval, Picasso, Apollinaire, Braque and the rest—would be driven away by the twin waves of speculation and tourism. The *butte is* pretty much given over to tour buses now, and it is as rare to hear someone speaking French there as it is to find a decent restaurant. No matter. The old village is still beautiful; and Place du Tertre, on the top of the hill, is like a sympathetic, vest-pocket image of the Paris we all carry in our dreams, even if it is thronged by Japanese, American and Serbo-Croat tourists all vying with one another to buy the same genuine Matisse from the same fly-by-night hustlers.

The casual visitor rarely takes the trouble to walk downhill—among any of the dozens of cobbled lanes, or via the many stairways—or even use the funicular to reach Rue Lepic or Rue Caulaincourt or Rue Marcadet. That's a pity. Each block is like a self-sufficient unit, with its own bakery, butcher, haberdashery, *crémerie, épicerie* and, naturally, a café or two. This is the sort of Paris in which Georges Simenon placed his Inspector Maigret time and again, ruminatively gazing into courtyards, questioning *concierges*, quaffing a beer with his sauerkraut or *daube de boeuf* at a neighbourhood restaurant. Simenon is one of the greatest writers when it comes to describing the Paris of the little people. His Maigret novels help us to understand how there can still be, even today, old couples on the *butte* who virtually never leave the hill and who, if they do leave, refer to the trip as "going down to Paris".

It is much the same on the next hill to the east, across the steel barriers formed by the tracks sweeping away from Gare du Nord and Gare de l'Est, and just beyond Parc des Buttes-Chaumont, that most picturesque of Paris parks. This is one of my favourite areas of Paris, on the outskirts of industrial Belleville but still untouched by skyscrapers and as unknown to foreigners as it is to most Parisians. There, on streets named Liberté, Fraternité and Egalité, cluster hundreds of the tiny two-storey houses the French call *pavillons* (if you are a worker, you live in a *pavillon*; if you are a bourgeois, it is a *villa*). These little houses are separated by concrete walks and minuscule patches of green. Of the most extraordinary architectural variety, they often are quite ugly, often close to laughable, but they are pure products of the Frenchman's passion for having his own patch of ground and his own roof over his head. Most of them, the passer-by senses, were built by the occupants themselves, or perhaps by their ancestors; lovingly erected, brick by brick, over weekends and during vacations that were earned at some boring and demeaning job in a factory or warehouse.

Between Montmartre and Belleville lies a giant, sickle-shaped curiosity: the Canal St-Martin. It was completed in 1825 as a perfectly sensible short-cut by which horse-drawn barges, carrying virtually all the heavy freight, would be able to cut north through the city, by-pass the long, tedious loop of the Seine by Sèvres and St-Cloud, and rejoin the main river again via Canal St-Denis. Another arm continued north-east, became the Canal de l'Ourcq, and ran deep into the countryside towards Soissons before petering out 60 miles away near a town called Silly-la-Poterie.

For 30 years the canal was open to the sky and crossed only by six wooden drawbridges. Then, in 1860, Baron Haussmann decided that it bore a dangerous resemblance to a moat; by cutting or burning the bridges, the entire north-east section of the city, the sanctuary of the poorest and most disputatious bourgeois-baiting workers, could be converted into an easily defended bastion. So, Haussmann covered about half the length of the canal with stone vaulting and put a roof of paving stones over that section to create the present Boulevard Richard Lenoir, which runs to the Bastille. His logic was gallingly prescient. Eleven years later, in the horrible butchery of the Paris Commune, the last pockets of popular resistance to the central government—The Versaillais, as they were called—held out at the barricades in Belleville and the tombstones of near-by Père Lachaise Cemetery.

The Canal St-Martin is hardly ever visited today. It is not even listed in most guide-books. Strollers who notice it at all see only an arm of water that passes through a lock from the Seine opposite Gare d'Austerlitz,

A man makes his way home through slanting, winter afternoon sunlight that gilds the cobbled streets of Montmartre, which, until the mid-19th Century, was a small village outside Paris. The curve of the narrow street, reflected in the shop window at left, still follows the old line of the country lane that it once was.

continues to Place de la Bastille and then seemingly stops. In fact, of course, it extends very much farther. The few barges still operating on the canal carry straight on into the eerie darkness, under the Bastille. Sometimes they cross over the *Métro*, sometimes under it. (As with most other big cities, below street level Paris is pierced like a Swiss cheese.) Occasionally, they chug into brilliant spears of light thrown down from grilled openings in the streets above, and then they emerge into the open air for the last mile of their passage, negotiating nine locks before reaching the Villette Basin, where the Ourcq and St-Denis canals branch off at a Y-shaped junction.

The railroad and the automobile have virtually rendered the Canal St-Martin obsolete. Its still waters are rarely disturbed now, and only the few Parisians who care to visit this corner of town fully appreciate that the parklets built around the locks—Square des Récollets, Square Eugène-Varlin—are strikingly beautiful oases of 19th-Century charm and repose; quite literally, they are backwaters in the middle of the city. But the aesthetic value of this area in general has been officially recognized and— by leaving the water as it is, by planting grass and more trees along its banks—the City of Paris will acquire one of the most unusual and gracious parks of which any urban planner could dream—a perfect complement to the banks of the Seine. If we are extraordinarily lucky, the Villette Basin also will blossom anew, being cleared one day of its tawdry incrustations of warehouses, then planted and beautified and opened up to the public by the removal of the walls and barriers and fences that now block it off from humanity. In this way, it would regain the role it filled so magnificently in the first half of the 19th Century: a promenade in the summer and a skating pond in the winter.

Below Belleville, closer down towards the Seine, lies the former village of Charonne, almost as quaintly countrified as Montmartre but not, alas, as safe from the depredations of the promoters. As shabby and work-a-day as Montmartre is well-oiled and touristy, Charonne these days is hardly ever visited except by eccentrics or by entrepreneurs scanning it for possible profit. The centre of attraction, the focus of the village, is the Église St-Germain-de-Charonne. It is a typical old rural church of this part of France with dark, squat bell tower, heavy beams and a little cemetery on the uphill side, towards Place Gambetta. In the web of little streets that fall away from the church are reminders of a country life that seems to have ceased only a few moments ago: an ancient tiled roof, a cobbled courtyard with grass growing high between the stones, a lounging dog, a widow dressed in black peering suspiciously from behind a heavy wooden door.

Just south of Charonne, towards the modest circle of Place de la Réunion (where the *boulistes*—bowls players—are out in force whenever there is sunshine), the 20th Century thrusts its reminders at you with rather more

Cars line the streets of Montmartre and television aerials festoon the roofs, dispelling some of the old district's much-vaunted picturesque charm. But no change can obscure the dramatic visual effects of Montmartre's steep hill which falls away to the city below.

tiresome insistence. But take a quick turn down Rue des Haies or Rue des Vignoles (nothing more than old village paths paved over) and you come upon an odd series of blind alleys with some of the very best names in Paris: Impasse Satan, Impasse de la Providence, Impasse de la Confiance (Confidence), Impasse des Souhaits (Wishes), Impasse des Crins (Horse-hair) and Impasse Poule (Chicken). Farmers and bucolics named these culs-de-sac, not the slick city wits "down in Paris".

There are other districts of Paris that guard a similar quality of other-ness: the Batignolles area, for example, in the little known 17th Arron-dissement, which gave its name to a Manet-led school of impressionist painters; or the wealthier St-Georges area below Pigalle, which used to be known as "New Athens" because of all the music and stage personalities who took up residence there (it is still crowded with theatres, and the Folies Bergère is just around the corner, over on the other side of Rue Lafayette); or Rue St-Charles in what remains of the old 15th Arrondissement. None of these, however, can quite match the rural quality that you find in Charonne or Montmartre.

Equally distinctive, in their own way, are the *passages* of Paris. There are more than 300 of these arcade-style thoroughfares, and I only regret that I haven't explored them all—because they add another colour to the wildly varied palette of the city, one that is different from all the others because never are there automobiles in these byways. And they have another distinction. The Galleria in Milan is immense and probably more beautiful, Burlington Arcade in London is indubitably cleaner, and the great Bazaar in Istanbul is certainly more colourful, but the *passages* of Paris are, to my knowledge, the only ones that have been immortalized by a great book. Louis-Ferdinand Céline's bitter, depressing and yet funny novel, *Death on the Installment Plan*, about growing up inside Paris and inside his own soul, was also about the inside of the closed, glass-roofed world of Passage Choiseul, a long tunnel of commerce in the 2nd Arrondissement, between the Opéra and the Bibliothèque Nationale. For the little boy in that novel, life in a *passage* was oppressive, and barren— years without seasons in a cramped shop-apartment that had flimsy walls and outside it only the filtered fish-bowl light of a sky forever sealed away. But in the context of the whole city, the *passages* are a new note, a surprise and an unexpected treat.

Paris, more than most cities, abounds with curiosities to be discovered at almost every turn. Some of them are historical, others, purely frivolous— yet, all the more enjoyable because of it. Like a Wallace Fountain, for example. Sir Richard Wallace was an English philanthropist and ardent Francophile who personally financed ambulances for the French armies engaged in the disastrous war of 1870. Later he turned his attention to the poor people of Paris. In particular, he was concerned that many of them

Seen through a wrought-iron grille above its entrance, Passage Choiseul, one of the city's many narrow arcades of shops, stretches from Rue des Petits-Champs to Rue St-Augustin near the Bibliothèque Nationale. It was built in 1825, soon after the restoration of the monarchy, when glass-roofed arcades such as this one first became popular in Paris.

had no running water in their apartment buildings and often had to walk for unconscionable distances to public fountains or else buy water from one of the *porteurs d'eau à la bretelle.* The *porteurs* filled their wooden buckets from the Seine or at springs and hung them from a leather "suspender" on their shoulders, ambling through the streets and crying "*A la fraîche qui veut boire*" (roughly: "Here's cold water for you to drink"). Wallace's answer was to pay for the installation of a hundred cast-iron drinking fountains that ran permanently with cool water and had metal drinking cups on chains attached to them.

Naturally, the cups have long since disappeared, but the Wallace Fountains survive in various parts of Paris. Pleasantly Baroque fantasies that reflect the taste of the times, they all take the form of four ample maidens—the Four Graces—loosely draped in togas that seem ready to fly away at the least whisper of wind, supporting on their iron heads a cupola, from the centre of which descends a slim jet of water. Seventy of the original Wallace Fountains survive, and it appears that they will never suffer the ignoble fate visited upon those other monuments of cast-iron utility, the *pissoirs.*

Paris, of course, bristles with showpiece fountains: arty creations like the Fontaine des Quatre Saisons on Rue de Grenelle, the Fontaine des Quatre Évêques in Place St-Sulpice, the Fontaine de l'Observatoire with figures of the Four Quarters of the Globe, and the Fontaine des Innocents, that 16th-Century masterpiece standing by Rue Berger, where the city's principal burial ground was once sited. But a more interesting, although less publicized fountain is situated in the west towards the Bois de Boulogne, in the ritzy confines of the 16th Arrondissement, where we find the city's highest percentage of rich folk and thieves. There, I often enjoy taking my ease on one of the benches of little Square Lamartine and watching the spectacle of The Fountain. This is no fire hydrant, no vulgar Wallace water-pipe, no mere decorative piece of statuary. It is The Fountain, La Fontaine Lamartine—only a tiny fragment of the "secret" Paris, but one I like above all because I find it especially significant of the French. It gets them in their two weakest spots—their livers and their pocketbooks.

Every French person believes, with unshakeable conviction, that normal water is as dangerous for the human organism as red wine is good for it. That the country enjoys the world's highest rate of alcoholism, I reproach them not; any people, whether they may be Bessarabians, Pomeranians or Icelanders, would suffer similarly if they had the soil and climate to produce such a plethora of fantastic wines. No, what I find amusing is the passion of the French for bottled mineral water. There are almost as many varieties as there are of wine; but whatever their chemical breakdown, they all possess one cardinal quality: they are "good for the liver". And the liver always needs help, the French are convinced, because half of what they eat causes liver problems—*crises de foie.*

Now, in spite of the fact that Paris tap water, drawn from distant rivers, is pure and delicious, the crystal emanation of La Fontaine Lamartine is particularly prized because it is true mineral water, the permanent flow of an artesian well 1,926 feet deep, originally dug in 1866 to sustain the lakes of the Bois de Boulogne but then turned over to the public. It is also free. The result of these circumstances is that La Fontaine Lamartine is under constant siege by a queue of hydrophiles that comprises as accurate a cross-section of the city's population as you will see anywhere. The *concierge* will be there in her slippers and dressing gown; so will the "monsieur" who lives above her, the taxi-driver from Belleville or the shop-girl from the Champs-Élysées. They all parade here with their thermos jugs, their plastic containers, their empty Jeroboams and their plain old water bottles; and the best part of all is that the *Laboratoire du Contrôle des Eaux de la Ville de Paris* has officially classed the water as *non-potable*.

La Fontaine Lamartine is certainly a curiosity, but when it comes to surprises I know of absolutely nothing that can match the *buffet* of Gare de Lyon. It is common knowledge that the city is served by six main railroad stations, and that inside each one there is a *buffet*, or restaurant. Yet millions of travellers pass through the Gare de Lyon to board their trains for Melun, Fontainebleau, Lyon or Nice without ever realizing that they are passing under one of the most extraordinary sights in Paris. The *buffet* is one flight up from the main waiting-room, and there is no eating place in the world quite like it. I may not be qualified to speculate about what Paradise looks like, but I have a strong suspicion that at least one corner of it bears a resemblance to this immense hall.

Overwhelmed by its visual attractions, I almost stumbled headlong into a hat-rack the first time I walked through the *buffet*'s heavenly portals. The décor, dating to 1900 and periodically cleaned and touched up, is so astonishingly sumptuous, the architecture so overwhelming, that life seems to take on a new dimension, complete with self-generated celestial music. This must surely be what an LSD experience is like. To the right and left soar walls covered to the last square inch with creamy, sculptured panelling and gilded wood, plaster and ironmongery. The windows—ranks of proscenium arches—are framed by heavy red velvet and embellished by spider-web filagrees of Auvergne lace. The gold-and-pearl chandeliers throw soft luminescences over brilliantly coloured frescos allegorically representing the French provinces. The art is so naïvely, and yet so gloriously, pretentious that the scenes become beautiful in spite of themselves.

Everything fits. The female bodies suspended by their backsides from the arch of the ceiling look positively luscious, like a mad *pâtissier's* construction of *crème fraîche*, raspberries and *fromage blanc*. The overall effect is stunningly dream-like. It is some sort of zenith of the Belle Époque, of a self-conscious and monumental art that will never return. In 1972 the

French government officially declared the *buffet* of Gare de Lyon a protected treasure and national monument.

Of course, many of the curiosities I have described here are of only passing interest and amusement to those who would like to learn something about the real Paris. For that specific purpose, echoing my earlier advice, I would urge the adventuresome but neophyte Francophile to walk through all the market areas where Parisians are down in the street buying and selling, because it is commerce that really explains the soul of this city. Napoleon scornfully dismissed the English as "a nation of shopkeepers", but he must have known, even as he was charging imperialistically back and forth across Europe, that his own soldiers—indeed, the entire population of his country—were *commerçants* at heart.

One of the most interesting aspects of commerce in Paris is to be found in markets like the Marché d'Aligre, tucked away in a tree-lined square between Place de la Bastille and Gare de Lyon. It is difficult to imagine what is *not* sold at Aligre. Locomotives and aircraft, maybe; but then again, you never know. Grouped around the *halle* of Aligre's central food market are the stalls, literally holes in the wall, of the Jewish and Arab speciality shops—alimentary coexistence in perfect harmony, with kosher chickens suspended next to *djendjlanya, frik, ras el hanout.*

Under the trees, neatly arranged on card tables or displayed on army blankets or simply strewn on the sidewalk, is the fruit of the labours of all manner of junk dealers. A few of the grander ones might actually call themselves *antiquaires,* but everyone knows they are really barterers, rag-and-bone men or—let's face it—*clochards.* What possible market could there be, I have often wondered, for combs with missing teeth, second-hand tooth brushes, dolls without heads? And yet the dealing continues, jolly and noisy and crowded, often accompanied by a desultory musician and invariably by the smell of food cooking somewhere. Sell a couple of old toothbrushes and . . . *voilà!* . . . there's enough to pay for a *canon* of red wine at the café on the corner. *La vie est belle.*

But it was out beyond Aligre—past the round, sterile Place de la Nation, past Boulevard Périphérique and to the very eastern edge of Paris at Porte de Montreuil—that I received my most indelible lesson in how deeply embedded is the instinct of commerce within the Parisian. My wife and I had arisen before dawn that day, driven by the curiosity to do finally, once in our lives, what smart French friends had been urging upon us for years: to go to the *puces* early, to be the first customers there and take our pick of fantastic bargains before the professional buyers arrived. The *puces,* Marché aux Puces, or Flea Market, is a great old Parisian tradition probably dating back to Lutèce and the Parisii. Most foreigners are familiar with the biggest one, at Porte de Clignancourt, but there are several others of smaller size but no less interest. This day we had chosen the *puces* of

Porte de Montreuil. It was a cold November morning and still dark when we arrived, shortly before 7 a.m. We then marched disconsolately up and down the empty terrain, accompanied only by the occasional discarded old newspaper skipping by in the wind and feeling rather foolish for our obviously exaggerated enthusiasm and wishing that we were back in bed like the civilized folk.

With the first thin light of dawn we heard a rattling in the distance, growing louder as it approached. Around the corner of Rue de Paris, turning hard right on to Avenue du Professeur André Lemierre, appeared two *clochards* pushing baby-carriages, those eternal vehicles of urban tramps. They had loaded up their perambulators after a night's beach-combing around town and now they were heading to market, hey-nonny-nonny, to find the best spot. Gradually, almost imperceptibly their pace began to increase. And then, in a moment, we realized the absurd truth. They were actually *racing* each other, galloping along over the cobbles, their landaus reeling and creaking like schooners in a gale, both of them hell-bent to snap up that good position by the wall where the bargain-seekers would be gathering later in the morning.

Could a few yards, one way or another, possibly have made any difference? We could not conceive of it. But then, as I thought about it later, I realized that their race was only in the logic of things. When you compete for business, you compete seriously. It was a matter of principle, that good spot. And there was one further little tag to our lesson that morning. No sooner had the *clochards* stopped and set out their merchandise than buyers actually appeared, just as our French friends had promised they would, materializing out of the shadows all efficiently armed with flashlights. Damned if I know where they came from.

6

Gastronomy's Capital

Gastronomy marches serenely at the head of civilization.—Marie-Antoine Carême.

A poem never was worth a dinner.—Joseph Berchoux.

How serious are the French about food? Those two little quotes—the first uttered by a cook, the second by a poet—are in themselves a pretty fair indication, but there's rather more to it than that. Everyone in France knows about Vatel, the *maître d'hôtel* at the Château de Chantilly, who in 1671 ran himself through with his sword because he had not been able to provide enough roasts and fish for a banquet in honour of Louis XIV. But more recently, in the mid-1960's, the chef of a Parisian restaurant named Le Relais des Porquerolles blew his brains out after the *Guide Michelin* downgraded him from two stars to one, and then to none.

Less dramatically, you can see the same seriousness demonstrated any day you go to market in Paris and talk with the tradesmen. I can't count the number of times my wife or I have engaged in learned conversation with the poultry man about the best way to prepare *poule au pot*, or with the butcher about how to accommodate a cheap cut of upper lamb ribs. Naturally the tradesmen all know dozens of recipes. But the best demonstration of that seriousness is in the restaurants of Paris, the exploring of which is one of the greatest rewards of living in this glorious city.

The same reminders are there in the tiniest bistro, or the most elegant, astronomically priced dining palaces: the style is different, but the basic meaning is the same. Take, for example, the intransigent manner of Claude Peyrot, who founded his restaurant the Vivarois on Avenue Victor Hugo around the same time that Le Relais des Porquerolles was losing its stars and its chef. Peyrot would not hesitate to contradict customers if he thought they were ordering incorrectly and might turn others away from his door if at first glance they struck him as vulgar or philistine. This is in the noble tradition established by the great Fernand Point. Shortly after the Second World War, Point became famous overnight for throwing a group of Americans out of his restaurant, La Pyramide, in the town of Vienne. Their offence had been to order Coca-Cola with their meals. Of course Point would throw them out; the customer is *not* always right.

Throughout my days in Paris, I have had innumerable reminders of the depth of this seriousness about food. Two experiences with chefs stand out: one, when I went shopping with Gilbert le Coze, the other, when I heard Alain Senderens refer to himself as a saint. I'll start the stories with my favourite "Saint of Gastronomy".

In the sumptuous atmosphere of Maxim's, one of the city's most famous restaurants, the élite of the gourmet world celebrate the birthday of a popular chef. Paris takes fine food so seriously that admired chefs can acquire the kind of "star" status that in most other big cities is enjoyed only by successful actors, writers and artists.

Senderens was only in his early thirties when he became recognized as one of the truly great cooks in Paris; indeed, a very plausible case was already being made for labelling him the *best* cook in Paris, but that is roughly akin to choosing the best 19th-Century painter, or preferring Schubert to Haydn. One windy March afternoon, Alain and I were sharing coffee above L'Archestrate, the restaurant in Rue de Varenne, that he had lifted within a few years from point zero to a gastronomic place of pilgrimage—one of the 25 or 30 finest restaurants in the Western World. As the afternoon drew on, possibly feeling the effect of the Italo-Colombian caffeine we were absorbing, he diverted his talk from the subtle tricks of preparing food to the torments and vexations of the money part of it all.

"You've got to have the sacred fire in this business," he said. "You've got to believe what you're doing—especially when you see people who know nothing, but nothing, about cooking making fortunes. I say the government should encourage us instead of raising our taxes. We're upholding the image of France. What else does France have but gastronomy? It's the best single thing this country produces. We should be preserved, like a vanishing species. We are saints."

Alain was so serious, so irreproachably sincere and single-minded that I found myself in perfect agreement with him. The one aspect of life that has most marked France, and that her gifted artisans handle with the most consistent skill, is nourishment in all its aspects. As far as I'm concerned, the best compliment one can pay this great and beautiful country is to sit down at a fine cook's *table sérieuse*—for some serious talk and some serious eating—throw away personal prejudices about food and simply appreciate the meal that the poet has prepared. There is no place like a French table for reconciling body and spirit to the anguish of a life that is necessarily too short and too imperfect, and there is no one like a good French cook to deliver that special peace.

When Senderens first opened his now-famous restaurant, he stunned conservative gastronomes by cooking his sea bass in the steam of red wine, then serving it with a red wine sauce. Fish and *red* wine—*quelle horreur!* That simply was not done. But this marriage of fish flesh and wine was so perfect, the sauce so unctuous, that his *bar au bouzy* (*bar* means bass and *bouzy* is the red wine from the Champagne district), became one of the most imitated dishes in Paris.

Some diners were positively offended to see a lowly turnip proposed as an *entrée* on Senderens' menu, but their taste buds tingled and their heads spun with joy when they met the subtle interminglings of taste created after the turnip was poached in Normandy cider and stuffed with aromatic herbs and meats. Senderens might cook turbot with tea, pullets with blackcurrants, and asparagus with caviar, but I soon discovered that he was equally capable of turning out a dish as ancient and ordinary as stuffed cabbage and giving it a special elegance.

At a Paris wine-tasting the faces of two guests appear tentative as they test the body and bouquet of a new vintage from Sancerre, a wine-growing district south of the city. All of France's wine-making regions periodically hold such tastings in Paris to promote their products.

My experience with master cook Gilbert le Coze was different. I first met this strong-willed Breton, as hard-headed and unyielding as the rocks around the island of Ouessant, when I dined out at Le Bernadin, his little restaurant on the *quai* opposite Notre-Dame. The menu was limited exclusively to sea food, and Gilbert, ever practical and scornful of superficial niceties, was tending his fires in a T-shirt instead of the usual chef's tunic. But no matter. As I soon found out, Gilbert consistently provided by far the best and freshest fish in all of Paris. This was not merely the impression of my taste buds. I *know* it was the freshest, because I went shopping with him. The market is now located in the suburb of Rungis, and six days a week, so I was told, Gilbert rocketed out there in his tiny car at 1.30 a.m., after seeing his last clients out of the door. "But I thought the sales didn't begin until five in the morning," I observed naïvely.

"Bah!" said Gilbert, fairly twitching with impatience. "You wait until the official sales begin and nothing's left but *de la merde.*"

We arrived at Rungis shortly before 2 a.m. on a cold winter morning. The fish hall, brilliantly lit by arc lamps, was a madhouse barely under control— ringing and echoing with shouts, with the clankings of pans and the polite whine of electric carts, and swirling with activity that was frenetic and yet organized as only the French can make it. For an hour and a half or so Gilbert and I stalked up and down the vast, frigid hall (it is bigger than several basketball courts), lifting covers off crates, poking dead sea creatures with appraising forefingers, warily lifting live ones, joking with a dozen red-faced dealers already heroically reinforced with anti-freeze, checking prices and generally snooping. Deliveries were still coming in. The retail fish merchants hadn't arrived yet; they would come later, for the official sales. Every now and then Gilbert picked out a choice crate or stole a single fish from a bunch and hid it in a corner under a counter. He was making his selections. One by one. Later on they would all be assembled for him.

Around 3 a.m., when Gilbert had just about finished, we ran into a *confrère*, Jean Minchelli, who ran another excellent fish restaurant, Le Duc, on Boulevard Raspail. The two men briefly compared notes (the *langoustines* were terrible that day, but the little live crabs were fine and the sea urchins superb), then separated. Gilbert chuckled sadistically under his moustache, like the villain in one of those old silent movies.

"I got the only four good sea bass in the whole place," he said. "There's nothing left but *de la merde.*"

That's one way to measure how serious the French are about food. I can't think of any other trade, anywhere else, where the craftsmen work with such pleasure and resolve. Apparently it has always been that way with cooking in France. But the accent has not always been on refinement. Far from it. Those early Romans who built Lutèce into a booming garrison town were quite amazed at the nutritional capacity of the proto-Parisians around them. Septimus Severus, that scholarly, much-travelled emperor of Rome (A.D. 193 to 211) is on record as saying: "Eating a lot is gourmandise for the Greeks, but natural for the Gauls."

While the decadent Romans were lying about, ludicrously stuffing themselves with the most wicked, rare and ostentatious of aliments—farm-fatted field mice, ostrich brains, nightingale tongues—the tripartite Gauls sat down to much less frivolous fare. Wild boar was their preferred speciality: cooked whole, stuffed with garlic and brought to the table flanked by roast hare, chicken, geese and grouse. Gradually, though, over the years, the luxurious affectations and complications of the Roman eating style—as if somehow it were superior—began to infect the youthful Gallic civilization. By early feudal times, calves replaced the boars and they were served accompanied by capons and partridges and with carp swimming in coloured gelatines as well. Now showmanship counted more than nourishment. At seigneurial tables the fashion was for immense constructions of dough and sugar-plaster, carried in on the shoulders of lackeys and then opened to reveal well-planned surprises: live birds that took flight, fountains of wine, pantomimists, even musicians tootling tunes.

When Clement VI was crowned rump-pontiff in Avignon on May 19, 1342, the *paste* lugged to his table contained a whole deer and a wild boar. Wasn't that a dainty thing to set before a pope? And in the entr'actes between these kinds of display, there came lesser dishes heaped up on huge trays, in jiggly pyramids of fish, game, roasts, ragouts, sauces and heaven knows what else. Diners dived in with hunting knives, pieces of unleavened bread, with their very fists. Paris, of course, led the way in this extravagant banqueting.

From the writings of Guillaume Tirel we have a clear picture of the strange fashions of 14th-Century French cooking. Tirel, known as "Taillevent" (a great Parisian restaurant, on Rue Lamennais, honours his memory today), was First Cook to King Charles V. Late in life, probably around 1380, Tirel put pen to paper—or, rather, quill to vellum—and composed *Le Viandier*.

Some historians have called this book the beginning of French gastronomy; if so, it does not give the taste buds much cause for rejoicing. Tirel always boiled meat before roasting, used bread dough to thicken his sauces, and over-spiced and over-sugared to the extent that hardly anything could have been left of the original flavours. Sugar was in such fashion in those days that cooks like Tirel did not hestitate to use it when preparing fish! Peacocks and swans were the most sought-after birds for festive tables because they looked the most impressive when painstakingly "reconstituted", feather by feather, after cooking. Solemnly carried to the prince by ladies-in-waiting, the big birds were further enhanced by gilding their beaks and feet. On special occasions a piece of burning camphor was

At the Barbès-Rochechouart fish market near Montmartre, one of many in Paris, an intent merchant cuts the remaining flesh from a large, half-carved tuna. The discerning palates of Parisians and the pride of such tradesmen as this one ensure that fish bought in the city is almost always fresh and of high quality.

stuck in their beaks, to create a delicacy called "Flame-spitting peacocks".

The second wave of influence from the Italian peninsula was infinitely more beneficial to French food than had been the inanities introduced by the Romans. It came in the form of a 14-year-old girl, Catherine de' Medici, who arrived in Paris from Florence in 1533 as the bride of the young man who was to become King Henri II. Catherine, who was no mean trencher-person, rightfully mistrusted the gastronomic barbarians on the other side of the Alps; she assured herself of decent eating by bringing with her a retinue of Florentine chefs, along with her royal perfumers, astrologers, ladies-in-waiting, lackeys and advisers. The noblemen who accompanied her from Italy soon sent for *their* chefs (presumably after tasting flame-spitting peacock or sugared fish) and good food became the court rage.

Parisians had at last discovered, from their subtler Italian *confrères*, a sense of measure and refinement—although they did not discover the fork until the reign of King Henri III, and it did not come into general use until the reign of Louis XV. Catherine brought unheard-of elegance to the table setting; guests ate from glazed plates, drank from crystal glasses and were entertained by ballet dancers and musicians. Still, she was not altogether free from her own manner of excess. At one feast "she ate so much that she almost died. . . . It was said that she had eaten too many artichoke hearts and roosters' combs and kidneys, of which she was most fond".

Within a few years the court chefs in Paris completely outstripped their Italian teachers and truly opened the era of *la cuisine française* as the symbol and standard of unsurpassed culinary quality. By 1550 the Maréchal de Vieilleville was crowing: "No other kings in Christendom, or even of the universe, can approach our excellent delicacies."

Paris' good King Henri IV enjoyed eating so much that he often lent a hand in the royal vegetable garden and prepared his own soups and salads in the kitchen. In 1599 he gave his nation's cooks official status by creating the *Corporation des Cuisiniers*, the cooks' guild. And so certain was he of the benefits of *gourmandise* that once, when he fell seriously ill with a high fever, he invented a cure for himself (against his physicians' protests) by eating large doses of sardines and oysters on the half shell, and washing them down with spice-wine. He survived both the fever and the cure.

Nor was good eating restricted to the nobility. Girolamo Lippomano, the Venetian ambassador to Paris, observed that "pork is the customary meat of poor people, but only of those who are truly poor. Every worker, every merchant, however wretched he may be, intends to have mutton, venison or partridge on meat days, just like the rich; on lean days [he has] salmon, codfish, salted herring from the Netherlands in very great abundance".

In those times Parisians nourished themselves five times a day: a bowl of soup or milk upon awaking; breakfast of bread and meat a while later, eaten "on the thumb" with one's personal knife; dinner, the day's main meal, around 1 or 2 p.m.; *goûter* (tasting) around six o'clock; finally, *souper* just before the candles were snuffed out at 9 p.m. or so. If this strikes modern readers as a lot, it was nothing compared with what was consumed daily at Versailles. Like Henry VIII of England, Louis XIV was renowned for his gluttony. The Sun King was the No. 1 eater in a nation of eaters, and there are numerous references to his bulimia. "An immense and varied crowd gathers 'round," wrote Saint-Simon, a nobleman and memorialist who was part of the Versailles court, "to admire the exquisite politeness and perfect etiquette with which he swallows a *compote*, a chunk of veal, a huge salad, three partridges, a carp, a frangipane tart and preserved fruits."

After Louis XV, a true gourmet and an intelligent eater, our hapless friend Louis XVI continued the Sun King's honoured table traditions, but without any of his grandeur. On his wedding day in May of 1770 he "ate himself breathless". His grandfather, perhaps thinking of the trials of the bridal chamber, gently admonished him not to charge his stomach too heavily. "Why not?" burbled Louis in reply. "I sleep so much better when I have supped well." On the day the revolutionary tribunal ordered him guillotined, Louis heard the sentence, then returned to his cell to devour six cutlets, a large portion of chicken and some eggs, accompanied by two glasses of French wine and one of Spanish. Then he slept.

With all its puritanical aspects, it was the Revolution that was responsible for the flowering of *la cuisine française*. The destruction of the privileges of the aristocracy left hundreds of private chefs out of work; many of them

In the wine cellar of a Paris bistro, a dedicated caviste (cellar-man), using old, traditional techniques, seals bottle tops with wax. Such seals, originally devised to deter rats and weevils from eating into the corks, are rarely used now. Instead, the corks are usually covered with lead or aluminium foil, a faster and cheaper method.

solved their problems by opening their own restaurants. It was an entirely new and unknown kind of business. The first restaurant in Paris, surprising as it may seem, dates only from 1765. Indeed, the word "restaurant" did not even exist then. The *ancien régime* had no shortage of eating places, to be sure, but without exception they were rough-hewn drinking halls where food was more or less accidental. *Cabarets* were "places of debauch" serving beer in pots; *tavernes* sold wine by the glass or bottle and had some food available, but offered neither napkin nor plates; *hôtels* were for sleeping only; *auberges* were countryside inns for the feeding and lodging of travellers. Meals outside the house were created only by the *traiteurs*, cooks who prepared food in their shops or at streetside grills and then delivered it to private homes.

It remained for a man with the fittingly food-ish name of Boulanger (baker) to make the great step of inventing an establishment serving food and drink at fixed hours, in a civilized manner and at separate tables. It was enough of a curiosity for Diderot to have written to a friend about "going to dine at the restaurateur's". This new word came from a sign that Boulanger had had painted above his doorway, in atrocious kitchen Latin: "*Venite ad me omnes qui stomacho laboratis, et ego restaurabo vos.* (Come to me, all of you whose stomachs are in distress, and I will restore you.)" Boulanger's "restaurat" was relatively modest, though, and it remained for a certain Antoine Beauvilliers, a former cook for the Count of Provence, to open the first elegant dining establishment, near Palais-Royal.

Over the years the "restaurats", gradually became known as "restaurants", and they sprang up all over the city. It was truly an idea whose time had come, and Parisians flocked to them as if by instinct. Even during the dour, abstemious times of the Revolution, even during the food shortages, they stayed open and stayed full. In fact, the Revolution provided the opportunity for some macabre entertainment. On October 27, 1793, the executioners of the revolutionary tribunal offered themselves a belated celebration dinner after separating Marie-Antoinette from her head. The restaurant was Chez Méot and the menu was turkey wings stuffed with *foie gras*, roast chickens, quail, larks and champagne. One presumes that they ate no cake.

With the *Directoire* and the Napoleonic empire—maybe I should say with the entire 19th Century—food became a science and a passion, and a subject of endless research and delectation. Perhaps it was the instability of politics, or the fear of wars or further revolutionary madness, or perhaps it was, as some psychologically oriented commentators believe, a form of repressed sexuality; but—whatever the cause—19th-Century Parisians threw themselves upon gastronomy with a seriousness and dedication that today seems little short of awesome. French cooking became so famous around the world that it was deliberately used as an instrument of state. Napoleon himself was a meagre eater, uninterested in food; but he

In the kitchen of Lasserre, a renowned Paris restaurant, the serious atmosphere momentarily lifts as a duck is sent on a final flight before being cooked.

designated his Foreign Minister, Talleyrand, and his Arch-Chancellor, Cambacérès, to be the nation's hosts and give four gala dinners a week in their Parisian residences. Invited to these dinners were heads of state, ministers of all kinds, writers, men and women of influence: in short, anyone who could, in one way or another, be useful or sympathetic to the French cause. These two imperial tables in Paris represented an apotheosis of a certain school of French cooking—the over-rich kind, insanely complicated and wasteful of manpower—that has never been surpassed since. And the undisputed prophet of that style of cooking—its Moses, as one book has called him—was Marie-Antoine Carême, an impossible, arrogant, affected varlet, but an absolute genius of the stove and possibly the most important cook in France's history.

Carême was the first to modernize cooking thoroughly, to codify its recipes and lay down a set of rules that are still largely valid today. With him, it is safe to say, truly refined gastronomy was born. But at the price of what pretension! Carême and the Carême school employed immense "brigades" of underpaid and overworked specialists, sub-chefs, assistants and apprentices to turn out not only mountainous quantities of food but also spectacular constructions of food upon food that were known as *pièces montées*—a clear throwback to the days of medieval pomp. The *service à la française* of the time demanded that all food be placed on the table simultaneously, like a *smorgasbord*, or an Indonesian *rijstaffel*, and arranged in the most elaborately decorative manner. Carême used to haunt libraries, sketch out copies of Greek temples or English grottoes, then go back to his kitchen and recreate them in dough and spun sugar.

"The fine arts are in the number of five," he was not afraid to write, "painting, sculpture, poetry, music and architecture, the principal branch of which is pastry." Take that, Le Corbusier.

Carême cooked for Talleyrand, for the English ambassador Lord Stewart, for at least one French princess, for Czar Alexander I of Russia, for the English Prince Regent who later became King George IV and, finally, for the House of Rothschild in Paris. He was the first to be called "king of cooks and cook of kings", a title also bestowed on Auguste Escoffier a couple of generations later. No one cooks Carême-style anymore, and it is just as well. The pompous *pièces montées* would appear ridiculous today; no restaurant would be able to hire enough personnel to make them, and hardly any clients, I imagine, would be prepared to pay for the assassination of the six ducks whose blood is needed for the sauce of a single dish called *oeufs à l'ancienne* (basically, no more than eggs in jelly—but very rich). Nevertheless Carême did leave behind him a vastly increased prestige for the *métier* of cooking. *Cuisiniers* were still developed from the "lower" classes, but now they were considered *artistes* rather than *domestiques*. More tangibly, he gave posterity five important books full of recipes and homilies, a veritable bible of *haute cuisine*. Most of these

Frédéric Delair, a former owner of celebrated La Tour d'Argent, Paris' oldest working restaurant, stands with a proprietorial air at the doorway of the then modest establishment in this photograph taken about 1890. Delair was the originator of canard au sang, the most famous dish on La Tour d'Argent's menu today.

recipes have been relegated to oblivion now, but every chef bears on his head a constant reminder of the old master: it was Carême who invented the *toque*—the high, starched chef's hat still worn in kitchens today.

While Baron Haussmann was gutting Paris in order to put it back together again in the imperial image, while Offenbach's optimistic champagne music was ringing from bandstands and music halls, while Daumier and Manet and Renoir and Degas were painting, dozens of great *artistes* of food, "the most ephemeral of arts", were creating their short-lived master-pieces in the restaurants of the Second Empire. Painters and writers in France have always loved food, but how they wrote about it then! A quick and, I am sure, quite incomplete list I jotted down one day of French authors who contributed succulent pages devoted to food had to begin with Rabelais, of course, but then went right into the 19th Century: Dumas, Hugo, Flaubert, Zola, Proust, Colette, de Maupassant. . . .

Victor Hugo was said to be a heroic eater, but he was also of the mish-mash school, mixing everything together on his plate—potatoes, vegetables, meats, jellies. Balzac, on the other hand, knew every restaurant in Paris, frequently described them in his books and absolutely delighted in patronizing them to the fullest extent of his incredible appetite. He will forever be enshrined in the hearts of poor, exploited writers for the magisterial manner in which he took advantage of his publisher in the Restaurant Véry, one of the best and most expensive gastronomic temples of the Palais-Royal area. The publisher took only a soup and piece of chicken. Balzac consumed one hundred Ostende oysters, 12 cutlets, a duckling with turnips, two roast partridges, a *sole normande*, desserts and a number of bottles of wine. And he made his publisher pay.

One French food writer has estimated that the serious eaters of the period put away 20,000 calories a day just to keep in form, and on special occasions would go well beyond that. The bourgeoisie had come into power now, and they intended to enjoy themselves as splendidly and indulgently as possible. Sometimes the enjoyment was surrealistically eccentric, like that of the glutton who disguised his capital sin by organizing an elaborate charade of imaginary guests; having ordered a menu for himself and six "guests", he would arrive at the restaurant alone, feign impatience with his friends' tardiness, and eventually sit down and eat all of "their" meals, served up one by one.

Still more eccentric was the Marquis de Saint-Cricq, a half-mad, aristocratic exhibitionist, dirty and uncombed, who customarily wore two frock-coats. He enjoyed his tea flavoured with salt and his salad with a generous sprinkling of tobacco, and when it was hot on the boulevards, he put ice-cream in his boots and drank ink!

So titanic was the eating capacity of some 19th-Century men of Paris that we have difficulty in believing their feats today. But the testimonials repeat themselves over and over again. One businessman ate ten dozen oysters every day of his life and hardly elicited a raised eyebrow. Why should he, when we have the reminiscences of Brillat-Savarin, a gourmet judge who wrote the great *Physiologie du Goût?* One of his colleagues, he recalled, had an unquenchable passion for oysters and said he could never get enough of them. Exasperated by this perpetual complaint, Brillat-Savarin determined to offer him a dinner beginning with a limitless supply of the luscious bivalves. "I held him company up to the third dozen, after which I let him go on alone. He went on up to the thirty-second dozen, that is to say for more than an hour. . . . However, I was completely out of the action, and since this is most trying when you are at table, I stopped my guest while he was going on full speed. 'My dear,' I told him, 'your destiny is to never have enough oysters. Let's eat.' We dined, and he bore himself with all the vigour and behaviour of a man who might have been fasting."

There is also the famous story of the Viscount of Viel-Castel, who bet that within the space of only two hours, he could devour 500 francs' worth of food in the Café de Paris. And he succeeded: 518.50 francs—for bird's nest soup, steak with potatoes, an entire lake salmon, a fat pheasant stuffed with truffles, a ragout of ten ortolans, asparagus, peas and desserts. To accompany it all he drank two bottles of Bordeaux, a bottle of Constantia (a celebrated South African wine), a bottle of sherry and a variety of liqueurs. It might be added that, as a gesture of bravado before the wager went into effect, the good viscount had begun his meal with 12 dozen Ostende oysters and a bottle of wine.

Why 500 francs? Because that represented the average annual salary of a manual worker in those days. Can we wonder how Marx and Engels ever came along?

While such excesses were going on, the poor people of Paris were learning to eat horsemeat. For centuries, even in times of famine, the French had recoiled at the idea of feeding on the noble animal; but gradually after Napoleon appointed a commission to study the use of horse flesh as a source of proteins for the poor, they came around to that recourse. After all, if frogs and snails and intestines and hoofs and snouts and testicles and brains can be made to taste delicious, why not horsemeat? By the middle of the century the step had been largely taken and the word *hippophagie*—meaning, the eating of horse flesh—had become a part of the Parisian housewife's vocabulary.

Parisians also took to drinking blood neat. Doctors in those days commonly prescribed fresh beef blood for the treatment of anaemia, and their patients would flock to the slaughterhouse at La Villette the way others suffering from *crises de foie* flocked to Baden Baden, Spa or Vichy. The blood was to be consumed hot, straight out of the animals' veins into drinking cups. The initial repugnance, it is said, quickly passed and was replaced by a perverse kind of enjoyment—blood was rather addictive.

As far as I know, Parisians no longer drink blood, but they devour horses with as much gusto as ever, and not for budget reasons. They firmly believe that horsemeat is a tonic—"good for the blood"—and the Monday horse steak and French fries are a typical part of the city's ritual, just as is the Sunday lunch, massive enough to stupefy a wild boar. Why Monday? Because many regular butchers close up shop, having worked Sunday morning, the busiest time of the week. Although refrigerators are now in general use throughout Paris, the Parisians have sensibly maintained their pre-fridge habits, and do their shopping daily, insisting on absolute freshness and scorning such hideous aberrations as packaged foods, mixes or that American crime against nature, the frozen TV dinner. On Mondays, when regular butchers are closed, it is to *boucheries chevalines* that they turn for fresh meat.

One last bit of macabre lore before we move on to more delicious things: it concerns the siege of Paris in the winter of 1870-1871. The victorious Prussians, who had defeated the French at Sedan and taken Napoleon III prisoner while they were at it, ringed Paris in a grip that grew tighter and crueller with every passing week. The city's fortifications held fast and prevented the enemy from actually taking the capital, but no food could find its way in. Soon Paris was starving. When all the normal supplies were gone, horses and rats and dogs took their place. The estimated 25 million rats of Les Halles were large and fat, and provided Parisian butchers with a thriving business. They went for about a franc apiece, on the average. But when they became scarce, what had to happen, happened: the city council made the decision to butcher the animals in the zoo. The resulting meat was sold through normal channels, and found its way even into some of the best restaurants, which produced such dishes as elephant consommé and roast camel English style (page 156).

With the end of the Franco-Prussian War and the installation of the Third Republic, the gastronomes picked up knife and fork and carried on where they had left off. But as the *nouveau riche* bourgeoisie grew more responsible and self-conscious, their gluttony became more and more a thing of the past. A new age of refinement dawned with the arrival of the second great French codifier of food, Georges Auguste Escoffier, whose writings and style of cooking dominated French cuisine right up to the Second World War. Escoffier's books (*Guide Culinaire, Ma Cuisine*) are still considered the grammars of the trade, but he was not without his pompous side and he is now blamed for creating "palace cooking", in which pretensions were prized as highly as the food itself.

Escoffier had a singular weakness for "current-events food", and so he invented dishes at the drop of a name. "Why a *pêche Melba*", a French food critic recently asked, "when a plain peach is so much better?" But Nellie Melba, the Australian soprano, was the toast (pardon) of the opera world, and so Escoffier felt compelled to make something in her honour

Aided by a burly assistant, a wholesale butcher at Rungis market, which succeeded Les Halles in 1969, expertly cleaves a beef carcass for early-morning buyers.

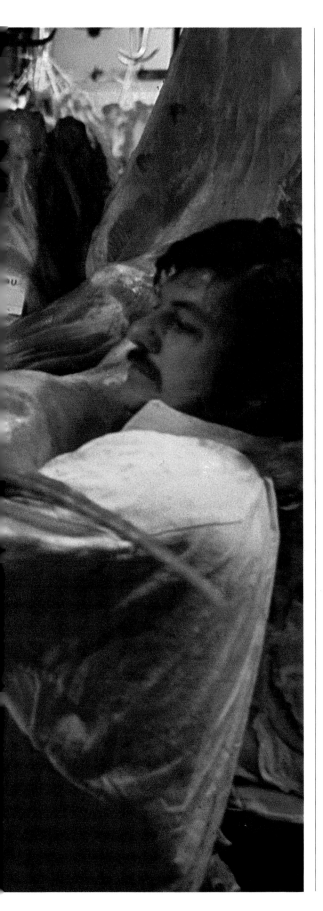

more sumptuous than the crackly piece of bread he had already invented to honour her. His nutritional flirting continued with *filets de sole Otero*, created to fill the undulant white tummy of a famous Parisian *horizontale*, a luscious tart named La Belle Otero. He pushed his fancy even harder (and, one suspects, with less pleasure) to come up with a dish allegorically reflecting the shipwreck of S.S. *Jeannette* on the snowy Arctic floes: cold chicken breasts suspended in aspic, the entire dish encrusted in ice. His worst service to gastronomy, though, was a bit of arrant flattery aimed at the Italian composer and false gourmet Gioacchino Rossini, whose lust for *foie gras* was well known. Escoffier requited it with *tournedos Rossini*, a bastard mix if ever there was one (truffle on top of *foie gras* on top of a circular fillet of beef on top of toast, the whole thing drenched in Madeira sauce), but the dish has so captivated indigent imaginations around the world that there is unfortunately no hope of exterminating it.

History is littered with examples of the Frenchman's fanatical regard for quality in food. Today we have the extraordinary good fortune to be living in one of the periodic golden ages of gastronomic excellence. Proof of this can be savoured in all manner of Paris restaurants, from the highest ranked to the most humble.

Perhaps a priest celebrating mass is more serious, and more ritualistic in his gestures than the *maître d'hôtel* I encountered at Lucas-Carton, the luxurious, classical temple of gastronomy next to the Madeleine. But I am not too sure. His name was Mario, and I took care to observe him as he prepared the *canard à la presse* next to my table. Into a curious silver vice — *le presse* — he placed the carcass of a lightly cooked duck whose legs, wings and fillets had been removed. He then cranked down the pressing plate until the last drop of precious blood had been squeezed into a silver vessel. Next he took a copper casserole in which half a bottle of fine red wine had been boiled down to a thick reduction barely covering the bottom of the pan — *une glace*, as it is called in the trade. Over the flame, Mario added butter, some *foie gras* and finally the blood, and it all came together for the most glorious sauce imaginable. Mario spooned it over the duck fillets, and it was time for communion.

I perceived the same seriousness when I first stumbled upon Le Petit Chouette, a name as slangy as it is ungrammatical, a hole-in-the-wall bistro on Rue de la Petite Truanderie (Little Knavery Street) around the corner from old Les Halles. What struck me then, apart from the picturesque front entrance and the fine old zinc bar, was the fact that most of the local Jezebels had chosen it as their luncheon club. These ladies work hard, and are *fines connaisseuses* of food; they demand wholesome nourishment, and not too expensive. How could I not love Le Petit Chouette, with flowers such as they decorating the tables? Especially when it offered a simple but delicious *pâté* from the Corrèze district, one of the best *steaks au poivre* I have had anywhere, and a home-made apple tart?

Nor will I forget the first time I set foot in Chez Jacques in the Faubourg St-Antoine furniture area behind Place de la Bastille. It was entirely fortuitous, my discovery, because I was hungry for lunch and just happened to be there. I knew immediately that I had come to the right place when I walked through the door and saw a customer—a moustachioed, fifty-ish businessman at peace with the world—tucking into an oxtail stew. He was holding the bone with both hands, eating the savoury meat the way an American eats corn on the cob. His eyes were closed. He looked like a big, wide, happy cat. I have gone back to Chez Jacques many times since then and I shall keep going back so long as they serve those *frisée* lettuce salads with hot cubes of salt pork (the lettuce icy, the greasy pork scalding), and the veal kidneys in a mustardy cream sauce so seductive that you could eat yesterday's newspaper with it.

Besides Lucas-Carton there are five other top-level "traditional" restaurants in Paris, establishments so venerable and of such consistently high quality that they have come to be monuments in their own right as familiar as Place de la Concorde or the Opéra. Of these, La Tour d'Argent on Quai de la Tournelle, with its spectacular view of Notre-Dame, is easily the most renowned. Indeed, it is probably the most famous restaurant in the world. La Tour d'Argent's 18 different preparations of duck have tickled such noteworthy palates as those of Edward VII, the Aga Khan, Sir Charles Chaplin, numerous French presidents and prime ministers, plus American Presidents Roosevelt, Truman, Eisenhower, Kennedy and Nixon. No-one knows how Lyndon B. Johnson missed out on this prestigious succession. Perhaps he preferred chili, a dish that La Tour has not yet mastered.

Le Grand Véfour on Rue de Beaujolais possesses what might well be the finest décor of any restaurant in town, a direct throwback to when the Palais-Royal was the great centre of sin, amusement and gastronomy. As for the other three, Lasserre, Taillevent and Maxim's, I must admit that I do not frequent them much these days, in spite of their uncontested excellence. I am waiting for an inheritance to come through first. Until then I will leave Lasserre (on Avenue Franklin Roosevelt) to the diplomats and to the knights of the expense account, Taillevent on Rue Lamennais to the classicists (it is the most *sérieux* restaurant in Paris, and its wine cellar is unequalled) and Maxim's on Rue Royale to the *beau monde* who care about who sits where and whom the head waiter recognizes.

If I have a franc or two to rub together, I will spend them at L'Archestrate or at Vivarois, where on my first visit, I was bullied by the tormented chef Claude Peyrot into ordering his fabulous *pâté chaud*. (More a meat pie than a pâté, it was constructed, I believe, of quail, partridge, goose liver and truffles, and was one of the eight or 10 best things I have ever eaten.) Or I might try my luck at Chez Faugeron where the wily, inventive Henri Faugeron was the first Parisian restaurateur to dare to serve his cheeses

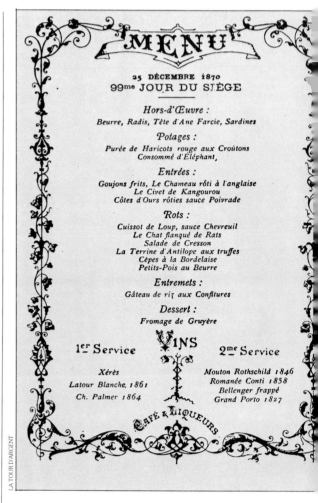

One of the weirdest menus in gastronomic history was presented by the Restaurant Voisin on Christmas Day, 1870, when besieging Prussian troops cut Paris off from its normal food supplies. The city's zoo slaughtered its animals, and diners were offered donkey's head, roast bear chops and kangaroo stew.

hot, on toast. "We used to have the usual big *plateau* of cheeses," he told me, "and maybe five or six guests a night ordered it. After I began serving them hot, I averaged 40 a night." Faugeron experimented on himself and his staff, and narrowed the choice of "heatable" cheeses down to only two: Roquefort and the little round goat cheese known as Crottin de Chavignol. For a while he thought that Camembert would be all right, but it melted and became rubbery and bitter. Out with Camembert!

If I had three francs to rub together, or a fairy godmother, I would be happy to luxuriate again in the famous *belons au champagne* of La Marée, on Rue Daru, the most elegant and probably the most expensive fish restaurant in Paris. I know purists will ask why oysters should be cooked when they are so good raw, but they would not be so quick to criticize if they could taste those firm *belons*, graded triple-zero (the biggest), poached in their own juices, then served on the half-shell with a reduction of their essences, champagne and *crème fraîche*.

Over at Prunier, near the Opéra or on Avenue Victor Hugo (there are two restaurants of the same name and ownership) the same irreproachable quality of seafood is guaranteed year after year by a family ownership going back to 1872. La Maison Prunier is so s*érieuse* about its provisions that a few generations back it decided to maintain its own fishing boat at the Brittany port of Concarneau. The land-based equivalent of that arrangement—a restaurant having its own farm—was later adopted by Le Récamier, a little establishment opposite the theatre of the same name and a favoured meeting place of Parisian writers and editors. Dissatisfied with the normal channels of supply, the proprietor took the simple expedient of buying a farm near Chartres where he could raise all his own vegetables, dairy products, poultry and pork.

Now that Carême and Escoffier have had their days, now that Frenchmen have finally come around to watching their waistlines, the accent of *la cuisine française* is more and more on lightness and finesse than on quantity. Sauces are used less and, when they are used, they are "shorter" —that is, less complicated and more digestible, thinner than the ancient *espagnole* (the basic brown sauce) or *béchamel* (the basic white) and all their derivatives. This new style, pioneered in the provinces by men like Fernand Point and Alexandre Dumaine, then refined by young lions like Paul Bocuse (Lyon), the Troisgros brothers (Roanne), Paul Haeberlin (Illhaeusern, in Alsace), all three-star chefs, was popularized in Paris by two remarkably successful gastronomic journalists, Henri Gault and Christian Millau. *"La Nouvelle Cuisine Française"*, they baptized it in the early 1970s, and the name stuck. Without going into too much needless detail, the basic tenets of the new cuisine are lightness, imagination and simplicity— "things should have the taste of what they are," as Curnonsky, the famous gastronomic critic said.

Many restaurants in Paris adopted the new lighter style, and almost all of them were influenced by it one way or another. The Vivarois became a proponent of *la nouvelle cuisine*; so did L'Archestrate and, in their own ways, such great traditional houses as Le Grand Véfour and Taillevent. More modest establishments also embraced the "new style", such as Le Monde des Chimères on Île St-Louis and the highly rated and original Bistro d'Hubert over near Place Vendôme. But for me Le Dodin Bouffant in Rue Frédéric Sauton became the most audacious of them all when it installed in its basement a large shell fish aquarium without parallel in any eating house in the world. With the temperature and salinity controlled, the water filtered and oxygenated, cockles and mussels and oysters and lobsters could live happily and healthily—if briefly—in their individual tanks, fresher than even the best that can be snapped up by the early morning buyers at Rungis. But then this restaurant—like the more expensive Le Pactole around the corner on Boulevard St-Germain—was founded by a first-rate *mauvais-caractère* of rare imagination and forcefulness: one Jacques Manière who won the admiration of all self-respecting restaurateurs in Paris when he threw a Michelin inspector off his premises for asking stupid questions. As a result, Le Pactole won the distinction of becoming the only top-level restaurant in the city not listed in *Guide Michelin*.

Whether *la nouvelle cuisine* is a valid concept or not I cannot judge; French cooking is so rich and varied and constantly evolving that I am suspicious of such simplifying labels. However, I am quite certain that gastronomy is now in a rare state of excellence. Never before have so many people willingly spent so much money in restaurants (in truth, they are too expensive), demanded such high standards or followed new developments with such interest. Naturally, most French magazines and newspapers have food critics on their staffs, and they are as carefully read as the foreign affairs analysts. Four major gastronomic guides are published every year (of which the best, by the way, is the *Kléber* and not the staid old *Michelin*), and there is even an annual guide to truckdrivers' restaurants!

No matter how fashions in food might change in the future, no matter which restaurant managers retire or which cooks pass on to that Great Casserole in the Sky, there will always be great restaurants in Paris, as surely as oil rises to the surface of water. But perhaps most amazing of all is the persistently high quality, day in and day out, of the Paris restaurants classified at less than the "three-star" level—those two-star and one-star restaurants and the simple bistros hidden in little streets where only the locals can find them. I'm not sure that a dinner is always worth more than a good poem, but I know very well that I would not trade the astonishing *cassoulet* at Restaurant Lamazère, the steaks or the beautiful, crackly grilled pigs' trotters at the Cochon d'Or, or the winy, overwhelming *choucroute garnie* at Brasserie Flo, for, say, one of the lesser odes of that 19th-Century English poet, Coventry Kersey Dighton Patmore.

If ever I have the misfortune to quit France it will take several years of diligent hamburger-chomping to make me forget the tiny, virginal grilled red mullet of Chez les Anges, the stewed hare at Le Grand Comptoir, the tripes at Moissonier, or the vinegar chicken at Benoît. And I don't think even a decade of Coca-Cola will make me forget Madame Cartet, one of the fast-disappearing breed of cooks who still labour in obscure kitchens to turn out what is known in France as *la cuisine de femme*: women's cooking. The difference between male and female cooking perhaps was best summed up by Paul Bocuse, who called women's cooking *"la cuisine de l'amour".* If it is less adventurous than *la grande cuisine*, it is also less flashy. And it is generous—how much so, I learned from Madame Cartet.

The first time I went to Madame Cartet's tiny restaurant behind Place de la République was for a business lunch with a colleague, to be followed by a full afternoon's work. I was amazed to see that her dining room was about the size of a corridor and her kitchen a closet. There were only six tables but they were filled, as they always are. Madame Cartet, looking more like a duchess than a cook, spent half her time at her stove, the other half helping her lone assistant with the serving.

"Here, try this."

We were still studying the menu when Madame Cartet spoke those words and plopped a huge dish of home-made liver *pâté* in front of us. A little later I had the temerity to ask about the composition of the stuffed shoulder of lamb that a gentleman next to us was enjoying. Quick as a wink, I had a portion of it on a plate in front of me. And so it continued throughout our lunch. The dishes we had ordered ourselves were copious to the point of folly, but the "extras" that Madame Cartet gave us easily doubled their volume. To this day I cannot remember what we actually ordered and what appeared on our table unbidden. But I do know for a fact that the two of us tasted a miraculous crab soufflé, a *brandade* of cod— an unctuous cream, combining the tastes of the sea with olive oil and garlic—beef *à la ficelle*, boiled with garden vegetables, two kinds of lamb, the best scalloped potatoes I ever had and three desserts apiece.

By the time we left, three hours later, I had a glimpse of what it must have been like for those amazing 19th-Century trenchermen. And I understood the truth behind an old French saying that I had never quite appreciated before: *L'appétit vient en mangeant* (Eating awakens the appetite). I never did get any work done that afternoon, and it was all Madame Cartet's fault. Somehow, though, I could never hold it against her.

Artists of the Table

By tables graced with fresh flowers, precisely folded napkins and gleaming silver and glasses, some of the staff of Lasserre await the day's first customers.

"The French are willing to spend their money on nothing so much as eating," wrote a Venetian visiting Paris in 1577, and four centuries later his words still hold true. Paris has many of the finest restaurants in the world—and some of the most expensive. The prices are usually warranted, for the city's restaurateurs have made cooking and serving an art that often requires small armies of highly trained employees. One famous restaurant, Lasserre (above), keeps some 90 people busy tending to only 100 diners at a sitting. In modestly priced places, where the staff may be only the owner's family, success is achieved through experience, imagination and hard work. If Parisians regard a fine meal as a near spiritual experience, it is largely because of the devotion and skill of the professionals who feed them and perfect the atmosphere around them.

In the early morning, freshly laundered table linen arrives at Bistro Allard.

Bread, still warm from the oven, is carried through Allard's old front door.

Plain Cooking Much in Demand

The word bistro implies cheap meals in a simple setting. At first glance Bistro Allard, featuring simple, home-style cooking and sawdust on the floor, seems to fit the bill. But its owner and staff achieved for Bistro Allard a reputation as one of the best places to eat in Paris. Its prices, like those of similar esteemed establishments, then rose well above the usual bistro range.

In the crowded but pristine kitchen, Allard's proprietor—just back from his morning meat-buying expedition—samples a soup prepared by one of his chefs.

Brasserie Flo's manager (right) personally prepares the day's menus while a cashier writes the prices on them.

At 11 a.m., before the doors open, employees enjoy a lunch similar to that which will be served to customers.

Preserving Flavour and Tradition

Brasseries offer less ambitious dishes and prices than restaurants that serve *haute cuisine*. But some achieve high status because of their specialities. Brasserie Flo concentrates on food, wine and beer (*brasserie* literally means "brewery") from Alsace, a French province whose taste is influenced by its proximity to Germany. Flo needs 40 employees to cope with its popularity, but still produces its famous onion soup and sauerkraut at modest prices.

Stained-glass windows, dating from 1880 when the brasserie was founded, are given their daily scrub. Flo's 19th-Century décor is one of its prime attractions.

A waiter in Le Grand Véfour, ranked among the greatest restaurants in Paris, carefully inspects a wine glass to make sure it is absolutely spotless. Located in the arcades of the old Palais-Royal, once the home of French kings, the restaurant has been in business since 1799, and has had its present name since 1814.

Lasserre's sommelier decants a bottle of wine with expert care, examining the contents against a candle as he pours, ensuring that no dregs reach the decanter.

High Style to Match Haute Cuisine

Lasserre, contender for the title of Paris' greatest restaurant, has special features worthy
of such a shrine of gastronomic elegance: impeccable Louis XVI décor and a ceiling that
slides back at a button's push to reveal the sky. It is not the setting, however, but the skill
of Lasserre's two dozen cooks and the artistry of its serving staff—verging at times on
unabashed showmanship—that keep the restaurant fully booked in spite of astronomic prices.

Aware that presentation is second in importance only to quality of the dish, a head waiter serves a speciality, La Timbale Élysée, with grace and flourish.

7

The High Price of Progress

"History rarely repeats itself," a Parisian journalist remarked a few years ago, "but rather often it hiccoughs." Especially, he might have added, in those peculiar places where human events have concentrated power and ambition and glory—places such as Paris.

During the imperial age of Napoleon III and Baron Haussmann, the City of Light underwent the most profound and dramatic changes in its 2,000 years' history. One century later that age found a curious distorted echo during the presidencies of General Charles de Gaulle and his successor, Georges Pompidou.

Each in his own style, those 20th-Century national leaders held the capital's fate in their hands just as surely as did Napoleon III and his ruthlessly energetic prefect. Their underlying purpose was precisely the same: to make Paris into a great modern centre that would attract money and talent and envy from the world over. Unfortunately, their approaches and achievements by no means echoed those of the last emperor of France.

Both Napoleon III and de Gaulle developed their theories and matured their determination while exiled in England—the former during the long trial of the Bourbon restoration, the latter from the disaster of the Battle of France and the Nazi occupation of his country. Napoleon III had ample time in his foreign wanderings to look and ponder and play the amateur urbanist. When he finally returned to power he actually brought charts and sketches and maps, filled with exact ideas for his new Paris. He was all prepared. Nothing was lacking but the right executive to make people and stone obey. When he located Haussmann, Napoleon III's plans were as good as carried out.

Napoleon III, for all his arrogance, had his prefect build a new city whose scale was human, where public services were vastly improved and where harmony and beauty—especially, the beauty of the parks he created for Paris—were considered as important as power and money. The balance of the Napoleon/Haussmann years must be considered favourable: the city needed modernization, and they accomplished it in an orderly and planned manner, even if they did fall into excess now and then.

Sadly enough, the same cannot be said for the de Gaulle-Pompidou period—the hiccough of history during which Paris underwent a second great wave of change. De Gaulle, naturally enough, was totally preoccupied during his exile with helping to win the Second World War and re-establishing France's honour; the city of Paris was only a minor detail of the vision for France he brewed over those cold, solitary years. It is doubt-

In a western Paris suburb, murals of stylized clouds cover the walls of 30-storey apartment blocks, called "Swiss cheeses" by some Parisians because their irregular windows resemble holes in Emmenthal. The structures are part of a huge residential and commercial development, called La Défense after a local monument commemorating the defence of Paris against the Prussians in 1871.

ful whether he thought much about specific details of street plans, zoning laws, public transportation and the like; Paris would simply be his capital, and his capital would reflect his philosophy. And so it happened.

In August, 1944, the general had the extraordinary luck to return to a city that had survived the Second World War virtually intact—a deliverance for which an eternal debt is due to another general, Dietrich von Choltitz, the German commander who had the good judgment and *sang froid* to disobey Hitler's vengeful order to burn Paris in the waning days of the Third Reich's power. But de Gaulle treated this precious gift with disdain.

De Gaulle is high on my list of anti-Parisians. He loved France, certainly, and never ceased to identify himself with its grandeur, but his character, his intellectual preoccupations, his very physical stature, carried him beyond the city he never understood into a lonely humourless realm in which he walked alone with his glorious preoccupations. "La France, c'est moi," he had been insisting *ever* since childhood. He never would have said, "Paris, c'est moi."

As much as de Gaulle was enamoured of France, he was less so of the French—and of the Parisians, not at all. Like Louis XIV, he mistrusted them and fled on every available occasion to his own scaled-down Versailles, la Boisserie, an undistinguished mini-château at Colombey-les-Deux Églises, a village in the flatlands east of Paris. A measure of his un-Parisian prudery is in the name of the house. When he took it over, the château was named la Brasserie (the Brewery). De Gaulle changed it to la Boisserie, which means, roughly, the Woodsman's house. It has a dignified, pithy ring to it, far more worthy of La France than "the Brewery".

But poetic justice always triumphs. In the days of de Gaulle's power I often noticed a particular little house on the road to his château. It was ill-built and rather dilapidated, this house, but it looked comfortable and pleasantly worn, like an old slipper. On the very limit of the property, right next to the road in fact, was that inescapable country accessory, the outhouse toilet. But whereas right-thinkers around the world name their residences Mon Repos or Dunrovin or la Boisserie, here it was the outhouse that proudly bore a title, hand-lettered in bold strokes of black paint on a tawdry old piece of board, in plain view of all distinguished visitors to the château. "Sam Soulage", the outhouse was named, *ça me soulage*, "What a relief". How vulgar. I like to think that the owner of the house was a retired Parisian. One does what one can to torment the mighty and powerful, now that *lèse-majesté* is no longer a crime.

In certain ways, de Gaulle even outbid Louis XIV in his anti-Parisian attitudes. At least the Sun King adored the sports of the table and the bed—nothing is more Parisian than that—but de Gaulle rose above them, too, in his sovereign misanthropy. He cared not a whit for food (the table of the Élysée Palace during his tenure was usually described as one notch above

MUSÉE CARNAVALET

The Place de l'Opéra, surrounded by the shattered remains of half-demolished buildings, begins to take shape in this 1860s photograph. The picture illustrates the ambitious scale of the alterations undertaken by Baron Haussmann, Napoleon III's energetic city planner, who reshaped Paris between 1853 and 1870.

a mess hall), and if anyone *ever* detected a Gaullian proclivity towards lechery, I have yet to hear of it. But that's all right: *Chacun à son mauvais goût*, as a Parisian friend of mine once observed—"each to his own bad taste". De Gaulle's offence was that he sat in la Boisserie or in the Élysée Palace, preoccupied with national and international thoughts, and allowed the jackals to attack the beautiful city.

The Paris that Charles de Gaulle inherited was basically Haussmann's city, but pleasantly touched up by the Third Republic. Enduring from 1871 until 1940, the Third Republic took culture seriously and allotted a generous budget to the *beaux arts*. Indeed, much of what the world knows today as the "Paris style" comes to us directly from those times: Hector Guimard's free-form "green noodle" *Métro* entrances; many of the old Belle Époque shops, department stores and restaurants; the picturesque Morris Columns which stand on the sidewalks like billboard-covered sentinels; the graceful steel arch and outrageously romantic decorative work of the Pont Alexandre-III; the Sacré Coeur Basilica on top of Montmartre; a great part of the murals, frescos and statuary embellishing public places; the elegant, spindly gaslight-type street lamps still in evidence in many quarters. On the surface at least, this was an optimistic moment of history, the period of Art Nouveau, of self-congratulatory universal expositions, of the Grand and Petit Palais and, of course, the Eiffel Tower. Altogether a good time for Paris.

The Third Republic's *bel optimisme* suffered a staggering blow with the First World War and died with a shudder at the Nazi triumph in 1940. The brief post-war Fourth Republic, concerned entirely with getting the country back on its feet, scarcely had a chance to make any mark whatever on Paris. That marking, when it finally came—and it happened with astonishing rapidity, like an overnight mushroom growth—was largely the work of de Gaulle and his Fifth Republic. By the time of the general's return to power in 1958, France had lost Indo-China (the humiliation of Dien Bien Phu was fresh in memory) and was in the process of losing its colonies in North Africa as well. More than anything else, de Gaulle was obsessed with restoring French pride and independence, with recapturing the *gloire* of ancient days. His reasoning was straightforward enough: France must become a great international centre of commerce, business and industry, and the centre of that centre was obviously Paris.

Because Paris is the premier jewel of France, the country's rulers have tended to look upon the city as virtually their private domain, a majestic kind of stone to be cut and polished in their own images. The laws gave them free rein. Throughout her history Paris had known many varieties of citizen's councils and executives, but they were almost always phantoms. True power lay with the sovereign. The city was governed from above, by royal whim, on the philosophy that the population was too intelligent and creative to be organized, too sceptical to be persuaded.

Long after the kings and emperors had departed, de Gaulle and Pompidou still held that old attitude towards the city. Both men maintained their own vision of Paris as a magnificent, throbbing modern metropolis, pregnant with French energy and enterprise, a model for all the world to envy. But in their haste to give flesh to this dream, they reduced their philosophy to dangerously simplistic concepts and equations: modern is good; old is bad; quiet streets are wasteful; skyscrapers are glorious. It was a strange, frustrating moment of history when French presidential aides and spokesmen, men of otherwise remarkable intelligence, spoke with haughty contempt of "museum cities" as they handed out thousands of zoning law exceptions to permit the construction of monstrous steel and glass office towers where people—usually the poorer people, of course—had lived before. Worse, the destruction and rebuilding was done piecemeal, with no Napoleonic master plan behind it. And there was no creation of new parks or greenery. Paris was being delivered over to business; humanity didn't really count. Beauty? That was for André Malraux, de Gaulle's Minister of Culture, to deal with. The best he could do—and we should be grateful to him for it—was initiate the clean-up campaign by which Paris changed her face from sooty black to the glorious rich tones of old ivory that she represents today.

As it turned out, de Gaulle never did manage to transform Paris into Frankfurt, Yokohama or Dallas, but he gave it a good try. The awful architectural results became apparent only towards the end of his time in office, but his attitude to Paris provided the climate. Out of their warrens crept the speculators, on to the streets, haggling, buying and selling, expropriating, lying and profiteering, all in the guise of "progress". Like the flocks of seagulls that follow ocean liners, the real-estate promoters—horrible little

A wedding party cavorts on a landscaped glade in the Parc de Montsouris. The 50-acre park on the southern edge of the city is one of several that greenery-loving Parisians owe to the bold, beautifying work of Baron Haussmann.

men in grey suits—coasted along in the wake of de Gaulle's monumental ambitions, guided only by that basest of goals, the profit motive.

It was during this period that the hideous word *rentabilité* (profit making) became a daily and urgent call in Paris. With *rentabilité* the password, offices replaced apartment buildings, and entire quarters were razed, dug up and replanted with mini-skyscrapers, or "towers" as they are known here—buildings as expensive as they were unsightly. The parts of town that suffered the worst were some of the most pleasant, precisely because they were the most bucolic and slow-paced, like Montparnasse, the near-by Rue Vercingétorix and virtually the entire 15th Arrondissement, where pensioners and artisans could still afford to live, where family shops and bistros were like village meeting places, and where the only fiendish machinations took place among the *boules* players on the squares. As a result, the *petit peuple* were forced to leave Paris in droves, out to the faceless sprawl of the new satellite cities, *les villes nouvelles*. Between 1954 and 1974, no less than 20 per cent of Paris' population left town, chased away by the high prices. It had become a privilege to live in Paris, one that modest salaries could no longer afford. And it has remained so ever since.

My personal symbol of the de Gaulle years is the Tour Maine-Montparnasse, 56 storeys of steel and glass offices thrusting upwards over the sidewalks where de Nerval had walked his lobster. The rare voices raised in its favour pointed out with pride that it was the highest office building in Europe. That is meagre consolation, indeed, for the "Montparnos" who walk in its shadow. They avert their eyes when they turn a corner and come upon its absurd bulk.

As for President Georges Pompidou, who enthusiastically shared de Gaulle's passion for grandeur, commerce and multistorey buildings, I have no idea of how history will judge his short administration (1969-1974) but for me he will always be signified by a stretch of asphalt and a single quote. "*Il faut que Paris s'adapte à la voiture.*"

Paris must be adapted to the automobile, he said. And that simple sentence so easily spoken, still gives me chills when I see it. Why should Paris be adapted to the automobile? Why not the contrary? It would be infinitely more humane, sensible and healthy. But Pompidou was a non-Parisian, just as de Gaulle was; a provincial intellectual with a Greater Scheme in mind. His approach to the city was reminiscent of the Auvergnat peasant who would unblinkingly lay low a 16th-Century stone barn to build another, of tin and plastic, in its place. To make way for the Voie Express Rive Droite, the automobile expressway that he caused to be built on the right bank of the Seine, Pompidou demolished the *quais* that for so many centuries had inspired artists, students, fishermen, lovers, *clochards* and other worthy citizens. Now the Right Bank Expressway is officially named La Voie Express Georges Pompidou and duly marked by a bronze plaque. It is a fitting memorial.

In post-war Paris, as in so many great cities, the civic planners were haunted for decades by one appalling challenge: the critical problem of preventing the city from coming to a complete standstill in the face of ever-mounting traffic congestion. It did not require any genius to recognize the need to extend the excellent *Métro* and open up new rail services for commuters. But I doubt very much whether even the ruthless Baron Haussmann himself would have entertained such a drastic notion as that of replanning his beautiful city to accommodate the automobile. More likely, his solution to the road traffic problem would have been to ban the private motorist from the central core of Paris altogether. The automobile, of course, is not a problem unique to Paris. The great mechanical ego-beast is basically inimical to all cities, when anything like generalized owner-ship is approached. Still, I do believe there is something truly unique about the relationship between contemporary Parisians and their automobiles, some unusual chemistry that is not present elsewhere. Certainly the motor car is something that must be taken into account by anyone who would know this city.

The newly arrived visitor's first deep impression is automotive. As the traffic swirls erratically around him he becomes aware of the terrifying combination of a Parisian's basic character and a powerful internal com-bustion engine. The private car is the instrument elected by the Parisian to even accounts with his boss, with his wife, with the very hand of destiny that has left him shorter than Charles de Gaulle and less handsome than Alain Delon. Moreover, the Parisian driver is so exceptional in his out-rageousness, so dangerously self-indulgent, that Frenchmen from Monte Carlo to Brest have learned to exercise special precaution when within striking distance of automobiles bearing that fatal "75"—designating cars registered in Paris—on their licence plates. Inside the Paris city limits, where all the "75" vehicles are together, the atmosphere in the street is like that of a barnyard full of roosters.

It is pure poetry: the drivers in their Renaults, Peugeots and Citroëns career around town at breathtaking speeds, flashing their headlights imperiously, treating traffic lights with seignorial disdain, making rude gestures at one another, slowing to avoid pedestrians only if the alternative is certain homicide. And even then the choice is not so certain. In my years in Paris I have read of at least two deaths resulting from fights over parking places. There is also a curious sort of formalism: since they have all been to *auto-écoles*, as required by the law, they are careful to signal before jumping lanes and forcing one another off the road.

And then there is the question of *priorité*. Ah, *priorité!* *Priorité* has afforded me some of my deepest emotional experiences, some of my most penetrating glimpses into the French soul. Who has *priorité* over whom is a subject of permanent concern here, and nowhere is it better illustrated than at Parisian traffic intersections. The single, primordial rule of the

French *code de la route*, the only one remembered at all times, is: *priorité à droite.* The person coming from your right always has the right of way, unless the intersection is controlled by traffic lights or signs. And *you* have the *priorité* if you are coming from *his* right.

Place Charles de Gaulle, formerly Place d l'Étoile, is the most commonly cited example of *priorité à droite* in action. This huge automotive pinwheel around the Arc de Triomphe is one of those places where, under the right conditions, anyone theoretically can achieve *priorité* over someone else. But I happen to prefer Place de la Concorde. It is faster than old Étoile, and for sheer terror value not even Niagara Falls or the North Sea in a tempest can out-score the sight of Concorde in full flood, when those intense, moustachioed faces, their dark eyes fiercely glowing behind wire-rimmed glasses, wheel their machines inexorably into the maelstrom, as confident of their divine mission as a 19th-Century English colonial civil servant, and taking their *priorité* at 60 miles an hour. Somehow those drivers already in the mainstream of the roundabout, coming from the left, usually manage to stop, swerve or slow down just enough to let the newcomer through before he, in turn, gets *priorité-*ed by another rocket from the next incoming road on the right. And so it goes on. The ideal, of course, is the four-way *priorité* blockage at intersections where there are no traffic lights and where, by a miracle of perfect timing, four cars arrive simultaneously and each driver has priority over the driver to his left—which means that *everyone has priorité!* The four streets then become totally immobilized, and nothing moves at all. It is Cartesian logic, logically confounded. I have seen only two or three of these pearls in Paris, but each one was so beautiful I could have wept.

One aesthetic notch below the *priorité* blockage is the *livraison.* This occurs when a delivery van — *livraison* means "delivery" — is parked smack in the middle of the street. It is in the middle of the street because illegal parkers have already lined the curbs on either side and now the road is completely jammed. Imagine the refined pleasures of the *livraison* flail: the serenade of horns, the fist shakings, the oaths and, best of all, if we are lucky, the *bras d'honneur* thrown indolently back at the blocked traffic by the deliveryman. (*Bras d'honneur: Characteristic Latin gesture in which the left forearm is raised towards an adversary, with the right hand or fist reinforcing it from behind. It is an expression of disrespect and is guaranteed to elicit a similarly contemptuous response.*) I would rather contemplate a good *livraison* scene than a Picasso painting or the entire Ring of the Nibelungen.

The concept of *priorité* goes far beyond traffic regulations. It reaches into a thousand aspects of daily life. Nowhere in the world is *priorité* spelled out so ubiquitously and so clearly as in France; this is a country where legalisms must be presented in their pettiest detail. The Parisian, unlike the Londoner or Copenhagener, is not civic-minded. For him, the letter of the law is necessary because he does not recognize the spirit. It is striking to observe that the word "fair" does not even exist in the French language. The closest thing to it, the word usually used in translations, is "loyal", derived from the Latin *legalis*: that which is obligatory, that which is required by law. The Parisian recognizes *priorité à droite* because it is law, not because it makes the traffic flow more smoothly. When he marries, he and his bride sign a marriage contract enumerating which possessions belong to whom. When he boards the *Métro*, his comfort and behaviour are constrained by a neat legalistic formula stencilled on the windows in clear yellow letters. Every foreigner visiting Paris has read it, and has probably wondered how any race could be so incorrigibly disputatious as to need such guidelines. But there it is: *Métro* seating *priorité* is awarded, successively, to:

1. *Mutilated war veterans*
2. *Blind civilians, job-accident victims and infirm civilians.*
3. *Pregnant women.*
4. *Persons accompanied by children under 4 years of age.*

On Paris buses a similar notice informs "*M.M. les voyageurs*" that the vehicle's windows may be opened, but that in the event of a dispute the *machiniste* shall give *priorité* to those who desire the window closed. And so it continues along one's mortal path—a confusing array of different coloured cards (all bearing photos, all marked by the impressive *tricolore* slash in the upper left-hand corner) that award *priorité* aboard public conveyances and in public places to different professional and social classes. An injured war veteran might be able to *priorité* a widow, for example, but in the right circumstances she, in turn, could *priorité* a student.

As I have suggested, this apparent obsession with rules is neither gratuitous nor accidental. Before stern regulations and guidelines were put into effect, an unthinking policy of *laissez-aller* had very nearly allowed Paris to be strangled by the private automobile. By the late 1960s traffic jams were approaching the scale of those of the all-time champions, the citizens of Rome; the pollution was horrendous and the sidewalks barely negotiable because of all the cars parked on them. Gradually, though, an intelligent policy of favouring public transportation began bringing order out of the chaos. The quaint, but still remarkably efficient *Métro* system was reinforced by a sleek young cousin, the east-west express known as the R.E.R. (*Réseau Express Régional*), which now carries commuters far into the suburbs. The bus system, which traffic congestion had reduced to near walking pace, was freed by the creation of reserved lanes, and the average speed of the buses shot up to all of six-and-a-quarter miles per hour. These lanes are forbidden to private motorists—a deliberate harassment that represents a heavy nudge of the municipal elbow, an encouragement to leave the cars where they belong, at home or underground, in one of the dozens of parking garages buried within the city or the even bigger ones on

On the city's outskirts, the tower blocks of La Défense, the biggest high-rise project of the De Gaulle-Pompidou era, dominate the view west over Paris.

the outskirts of town. Similarly, that dreaded killjoy, the parking meter, has quietly invaded most of the parkable streets, barriers now keep the sidewalks safe for pedestrians and—horror of horrors—the ticketing system for punishing violators has been computerized. All this is not to say that the problem of traffic has been solved in Paris. That would be asking too much of a French problem. But it has been brought within reason.

Taxis, too, are favoured over private cars (special parking ranks are reserved for them, and they are permitted to use the bus lanes), but they have not become quite so orderly and well-organized as the mass transit. After all, nowhere is the famous French individualism more pronounced than in this honourable old trade. The city has 14,300 cabs (as against only 12,000 in New York or London). More than half the taxi drivers are self-employed, independent "artisans", working with their own cars and in the individual style that pleases them. The result is a prodigious variety of machines and manners, far greater than in any other city I have known in Europe, America or Asia.

In Paris the majority of the taxis are French-made, but I have ridden in German and Italian cars, too, not to mention Swedish, Japanese, American and even Czech and Polish ones. Sometimes the taxi drivers bring their children along with them in the front seat, and even more often, their dogs. When the canine is malodorous and the cabbie hygienically negligent, the experience of a short trip is like a visit to the Augean stables. At the other end of the spectrum are the neatness fanatics whose speciality is to make passengers nervous. They are the ones with the sharp, bird-like features, the "no smoking" signs and the piercing eyeball gazing at you in the rear-view mirror lest you place your foot amiss and scuff the genuine simulated leather panelling.

Contrary to popular legend, Paris cabbies are almost unfailingly honest. If a visitor believes he has been cheated, I have found, it is usually because he does not understand the completely legal extra charges or the mysteries of meter readjustments. Naturally, such misunderstandings are only amplified by the language barrier. Unlike Stockholm, Hamburg or Amsterdam, Paris is not a city where taxi-drivers speak diverse languages. The French are so proud of their own tongue that they have never felt the necessity or utility of learning others. It is one of the difficult facts of life that the foreigner will never really get along in Paris unless he takes the trouble to learn French, however approximately.

The effort by which Charles de Gaulle and Georges Pompidou wrenched Paris into the civilization of big business and the automobile has created a city marked by a strange patchwork quality; a flawed jewel. Overall, it is recognizable as the city of Haussmann and the *Deuxième Empire*, but the style is garishly, unexpectedly, broken here and there by blotches of shabby, towering avant-garde growths (French modern architecture is generally bad), like weeds in a lawn. The "Front de Seine" complex below the Eiffel Tower stands over the river like a forest of plastic giants, parvenus strutting in the shadow of their older sister. The Porte Maillot convention centre at the north-western edge of town and, beyond it, the enormous jumble of high-rise office buildings known as La Défense, could be mistaken for Kansas City or Kuwait. At Montparnasse and the Porte d'Italie, around Gare de Lyon and, of course, at the top of the bluff by Ménilmontant and Belleville, the late 20th Century obtrudes so overwhelmingly as to dominate utterly its more modest, human-sized architectural antecedents. The futuristic picture is fittingly completed by the Boulevard Périphérique, the automotive speedway which, for all its ugliness, does circle the city to connect the various *autoroutes*, enabling travellers to slip rapidly around town without adding to the inner core's congestion.

While much of this rebuilding was undoubtedly necessary, a sinister sort of menace to Paris appeared towards the end of Georges Pompidou's tenure as president. Apparently fascinated and hypnotized by the idea of *le progrès*, Pompidou lost touch with the will of his citizens as much as he did with a sense of balance and aesthetics; transformation looked more and more like arrant destruction; one began wondering if anyone in power really cared about the soul of Paris, that part of the city that was concerned not with power or money, but with the quality of life. I saw with horror how far this deplorable trend could go when the Foyer des Artistes et Intellectuels, a sympathetic, dirt-cheap eating-place opposite the Coupole on Boulevard du Montparnasse, was razed and replaced by a steel and glass branch office of the Banque Worms. Of course it would be a bank. What else?

Around this time a premonitory article appeared in a Paris weekly magazine. "Why should out-of-scale towers dominate a city's skyline," it asked, "perturb the organization of the streets, and impose on the majority of the inhabitants the will of a small number of users? On the contrary, the city should remain familiar to everyone, and open to all the social categories." The author of that article was Valéry Giscard d'Estaing, the man who was soon to be elected president, after Pompidou died with his work unfinished.

I am convinced that Parisians a century from today will be thanking Giscard. Like Henri IV, he understood from the first that the city was for the people who live in it, not merely a machine to be exploited for the sake of the nation. In a very real sense he set out to give Paris back to the Parisians. One of his first acts as president was to cancel a strange project that had been one of the keystones of Pompi-Gaullian ambition, the Centre International de Commerce des Halles, an ultra-modern trade and business complex that was to have been erected on that choicest of sites, the vacant land just north of the Seine where old Les Halles had stood. Giscard reasoned that what Paris least needed was another series of towers in the middle of town, and he used the God-given opportunity—it isn't every day that a large chunk of free space is offered to a city—to propose that a 15-acre garden be laid out there instead, with several municipal services (*Métro*, telephone exchange, parking garage, shops, conference halls, etc.) buried deep underneath.

Across Boulevard de Sébastopol a few hundred yards to the east, Pompidou's passion for contemporary architecture is commemorated by the Centre National d'Art et Culture Georges Pompidou, a striking and aesthetically controversial glass box housing the Museum of Modern Art, a large library, a musical research institute, an industrial creation centre and other related activities. But Giscard thwarted a less tasteful Pompidou project when he saved, *in extremis*, the quays of the Left Bank of the Seine, which already had been written off for another automobile expressway. In the expressway's place he approved plans for a grassy promenade, ideal for viewing the two islands and the glamorous white flanks of Notre-Dame. And I add one final note of gratitude to Giscard for having saved the Canal St-Martin. Georges Guess-Who had approved plans to drain it and lay in its bed an eight-lane guess-what. Giscard strangled that turkey, saving the canal for beauty-hungry future generations.

By turning around the trend of unchecked growth and demonstrating a concern for humanity, Giscard, shortly after his election, proved himself to be far more in touch with the genius of Paris than his predecessors had been. In spite of the occasional abberations, Paris has always symbolized a concern for aesthetics, for proportion and for good living—for urban poetry, if that doesn't sound too pretentious. I like to believe that it will always remain so.

Paris of the 21st or 22nd Centuries may begin taking on aspects of those science fiction cities that illustrators are forever imagining—flying saucers, aerial sidewalks, buildings that look like light bulbs, and citizens in astronaut uniforms—but I would certainly expect that the qualities that have always made her so livable would not be neglected even then. I scarcely think that the cuisine or the *Parisiennes* would deteriorate; a French cook could devise a way to make an astronaut's nourishment pill into a sumptuous meal, and a *Parisienne* would know how to look stylish and provocative even in a space suit. The city's finer traits have staying power. Since the days of Abélard, roughly, Paris has been one of the world's five or six great seed-beds of learning and intellectual achievement, in the arts and letters as much as in the sciences. I would not presume to bear judgment here upon that vast field, or even begin enumerating its high points (I would run out of space before leaving the 18th Century). But we may be confident that, whether the subject is philosophy, theatre, painting or nuclear physics, the French will continue to add the wealth of their brains to the world's supply, and that it will be in Paris that this knowledge is fostered and most cherished.

Watching a swan glide past, a lone woman savours the dreamlike peace of the Parc des Buttes-Chaumont in north-eastern Paris. The boat is a hand-cranked, cable-pulled ferry that takes visitors to an island in the middle of the lake crowned by a copy of a classical temple.

Paris is propitious for these greater achievements because the lesser achievements support the men and women who create them. It is a city concerned with the everyday details of living, as much as with Great Schemes and Ethereal Concepts. It is for this reason that, although I am amused by the French approach to supermarketry, I fervently hope that Paris will remain basically a city of small, individual shops run by evil-tempered old ladies, however inefficient they may be and whatever price-gouging goes on within their cluttered walls. I would much prefer to pay 20 or 30 per cent more for a corkscrew or an apple in one of those shops than enjoy the low-low prices of the Shady Glade Commercial Plaza. To hell with *rentabilité*. *Vive la petite bourgeoisie.*

Will the 21st Century finally do away with the institution of the *concierges?* It would be cultural crime, I think, and Paris would never be quite the same without them. True, many of them are gouty old snoops; it severely strains one's dignity and self-esteem to be brought up short on a staircase landing with that imperious cry: "*Monsieur, vous allez où?*" But *concierges* have also defended me from fortune-tellers, preachers and lightning-rod salesmen, helped me tote furniture up five flights, baby-sat for me, delivered my mail, emptied my garbage and given me to taste of their own home-brewed wines and spirits. Everything considered, I would rather have one of these domestic dragons than a double-bolted entry-way, doorstep, intercom, TV monitors and electric locks.

And so it is with the Parisian police, probably the most maligned group in France, outside of whatever government happens to be in power at the moment. I have known cops in many countries, but none of them has been as smart, quick, polite and obliging as the Paris police. Because the police represent authority, they are the perpetual targets of the *contestataires* as a matter of ancient habit. "If I rip up a paving stone and toss it at the head of the first *gendarme* in front of me," a Parisian wit noted a while ago, "it is a matter of an honest dispute of principles. If he avoids the stone, picks it up and throws it back at my face, then it is a matter of odious police repression."

I can't imagine that attitude changing, any more than I can imagine an end to the hallowed practice of *la grève*: the strike. As long as there are two Frenchmen left on the face of the earth, one of them will probably be on strike. Sometimes *la grève* can provide adventure, as when the electricity goes off and Parisians dine by candlelight while, outside in the street where no traffic lights are working, everyone is *priorité*-ing everyone else.

More rarely, *la grève* may actually be profitable for the public. A few years ago the *poinçonneurs*, the *Métro* ticket-punchers, made their own particular *grève* while the drivers remained on the job. Everyone rode the *Métro* free then. But it cannot happen that way again. Automation has come to the *Métro* now and the automatic turnstiles eat the tickets without help from human hands. But the same exhilaration of getting something for nothing may still be experienced on the *autoroutes*, when the toll-takers go on *grève*. It happens with pleasing regularity.

The *cafés*, those irreplaceable places of meeting, drinking, talking or just looking, will certainly not disappear from the Parisian horizon as long as there is a litre of wine left in a vineyard or a sack of coffee at a dock in Le Havre. As they do in Italy, Greece and Spain, the cafés here incarnate the Latin passion for sitting and sharing the spectacle of the street—a pleasure virtually unknown in the Nordic countries where the drinker takes refuge, to sip his glass in silence in a dark room, separated from the street by plaster walls or plush curtains.

As for the larger question of the urban landscape, Paris had a good fright at the hands of the real-estate speculators and has reacted. The public, no longer cowed by official complicity with the promoters, has assumed the responsibility of vigilance against further depredation by cheque book and bulldozer. I am not certain that a soul can be saved by parks and trees and historical buildings, but I am sure that it can be lost by a surfeit of concrete and *gloire*. Now Paris has an *Inspecteur des Monuments Historiques*, and France has a Minister of the Quality of Life.

Even more important, Paris has her own mayor now. Previously, she had been run like a fiefdom of the Élysée Palace—a result of the terrible bloodshed of the 1871 *commune* when a vicious civil war was fought in the city's streets, leaving some 25,000 dead. For more than a century Paris was punished for that insurrection against the central government. Then, in the mid-1970s, the Giscard administration consented to loosen the grip of authority and allow a real city council and a real chief executive, both with real power. Paris took her own destiny back in hand.

Judging from my own years in this city, I doubt that this new responsibility will lead future Parisians to become any less complex, difficult, sceptical or intractable. I would be bitterly disappointed if they ever became "nice". And I couldn't reasonably expect them to pass any less time complaining than they do now, for it is one of their most profound pleasures. Everything considered, I suppose I would most like to wish sovereign, incurable inefficiency upon the people of Paris. Whatever wonders of science and technology the future might bring, whatever revolutionary new techniques of personnel and business organization, I trust that the Parisians will always continue to treat them with proper scorn and reserve the prime part of their energies for the things they truly value: food, love, amusement, children, and the creation and contemplation of beauty.

Old Sights That Are Forever New

The shape of its distant domes echoed by the rounded clouds above them, the Sacré-Coeur Basilica, a Paris landmark, glistens over the city from Montmartre.

Paris, perhaps more than other great cities, has a personal, intangible essence that transcends any mere catalogue of its visible attractions. The pursuit of this private Paris—which is different for each person—can be so beguiling that a visitor may find himself ignoring the city's public face. The Eiffel Tower, Notre-Dame, the Arc de Triomphe and all the other historic monuments and vistas have been seen in so many photographs and paintings that they can fade behind a glaze of familiarity. Yet it takes only a momentary change of light or single eccentric detail—a figure in the landscape, a richly clouded sky, a tender dusk—to rescue such well-known sights from the glib symmetry of the postcard views that trivialize them. Suddenly, they appear afresh before the watcher's eyes, and the timeless visual glory of Paris is once more renewed.

Notre-Dame (right) is eight centuries old, but seen from a rooftop across the Seine, its uplifting vertical lines and flying buttresses still appear architecturally youthful and vigorous. And as a pigeon flutters towards a perch (above), the cathedral's façade catches light that makes its ancient stone glow warmly.

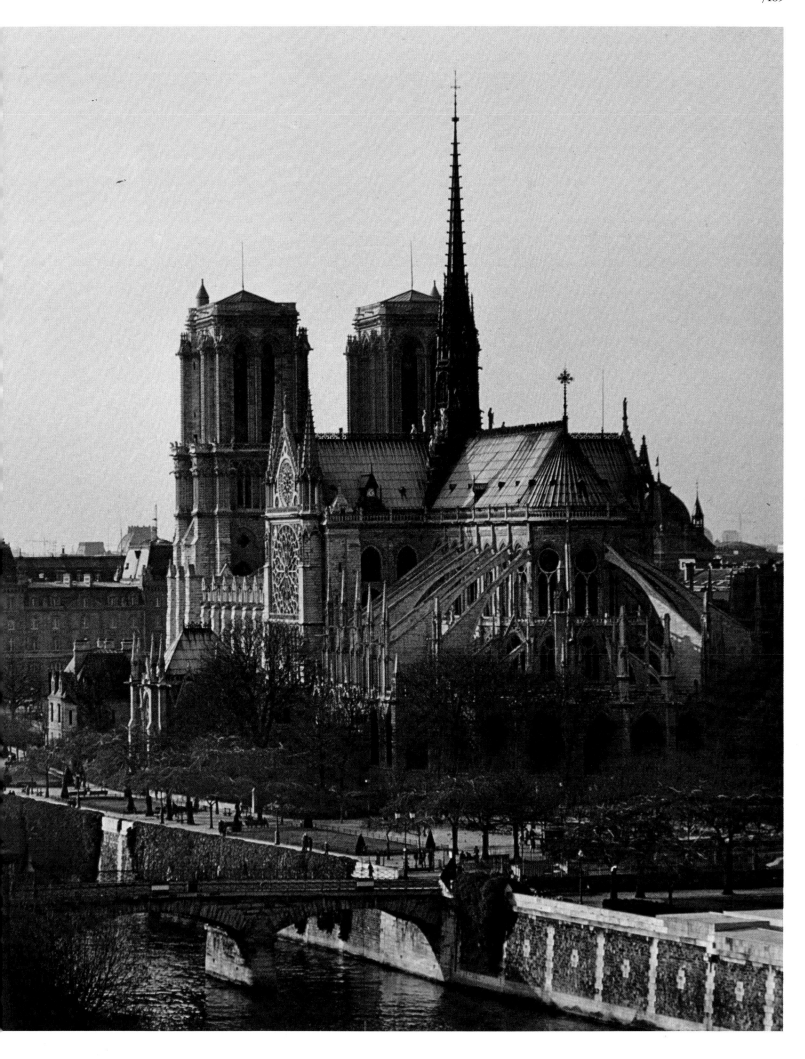

Orderly files of trees underline the ruler-straight regularity of the handsome 18th-Century buildings of the Palais-Royal. The hypnotic succession of identical windows is relieved only by the presence of a lone window-cleaner who is clinging precariously to one of them.

A dusting of winter snow between black lines of trees lends an alien atmosphere to a familiar perspective in the Tuileries Gardens looking towards the high, narrow end of the Louvre. The cloaked figure in the foreground, dwarfed by a statue of mythological figures, adds an impression of muted mystery.

Like strange but recognizable spectres, two of
the city's best known structures (left) rise
ghostly grey above the Paris rooftops: the
dome of Les Invalides, under which Napoleon's
body lies, and the iron lattice of the Eiffel
Tower. Seen from a distance, the Tower seems
a work of lace-like filigree, but from close
up (above) it is as sturdy as a railway bridge.

As night falls on the Champs-Élysées, the lights of cars on the sloping avenue suggest a red-and-white fireworks shower beneath the golden glow of the floodlit Arc de Triomphe. In the foreground, the slender shaft of the Egyptian obelisk in Place de la Concorde is silhouetted against the fading light of day.

Bibliography

Aron, Jean-Paul, *Le Mangeur du dix-neuvième Siècle.* Robert Laffont, Paris, 1973.
Bagot, Michel and Zoche, Jean, *Paris Guidorama.* Stock, Paris, 1975.
Barrois, Maurice, *Le Paris sous Paris.* Hachette, Paris, 1965.
Brillat-Savarin, Jean Anthelme, *Philosopher in the Kitchen.* Penguin, Middlesex, 1970.
Carroll, Joseph T., *The French: how they live and work.* David and Charles, Newton Abbot, 1973.
Chastel, André, *Paris.* Thames and Hudson, 1971.
Chevais, François, *Guide de Saint-Germain des Prés.* Horay, Paris, 1975.
Claiborne, Craig, *Classic French Cooking.* Time-Life Books, New York, 1971.
Courtine, Robert, *La Gastronomie.* Presses Universitaires de France, 1970.
Cronin, Vincent, *The Companion Guide to Paris.* Collins, London, 1973.
Dansel, Michel, *Au Père Lachaise.* Fayard, Paris, 1973.
Dubly, Henry-Louis, *Ponts de Paris.* Henri Veyrier, Paris, 1974.
Fletcher, Sir Banister, *A History of Architecture.* The Athlone Press, London, 1975.
Garlin, Gustave, *Le Cuisinier Moderne.* Garnier Frères, Paris, 1887.
Gault, Henri and Millau, Christian, *Le Nouveau Guide de Paris.* Agence Presse-Loisirs, Paris, 1975.
Guy, Christian, *La Vie quotidienne de la Société Gourmande au dix-neuvième Siècle.* Hachette, Paris, 1971.
Hautecoeur, Louis, *Paris.* Fernand Nathan, Paris, 1972.
Herchenroeder, Jan, *Paris—Get to know it, Get to like it.* Interauto Book Co., Brentford, 1972.
Héron de Villefosse, René, *Histoire et Géographie Galantes de Paris.* Les Éditions de Paris, Paris, 1957.
Hillairet, Jacques, *Dictionnaire Historique des Rues de Paris.* Les Éditions de Minuit, Paris, 1973.
Horne, Alistair, *The Terrible Year.* Macmillan, London, 1971.
Hürlimann, Martin, *Paris.* Thames and Hudson, London, 1971.
Laffont, Robert, *Histoire de Paris et des parisiens.* Editions du Pont-Royal, 1958.
Life, *Guide to Paris.* Time Incorporated, New York, 1962.
Michelin, *Green Guide to Paris.* Paris, 1972.
Mitford, Nancy, *The Sun King.* Hamish Hamilton, London, 1966.
Nitze, William A. and Dargan, E. Preston, *A History of French Literature.* George G. Harrap, London, 1923.
Olivier-Michel, Françoise and Gisler, Claude, *Guide Artistique de la France.* Éditions Pierre Tisné, Paris, 1964.
Ostrogorsky, Clara Westman and Davoust, Eugène-Pierre, *Ça c'est Paris.* Methuen, London, 1960.
Paris, Anne and Riou, Alain, *Paris Pas Cher.* Guy Authier, Paris, 1974.
Pillement, Georges, *Paris Disparu.* Bernard Grasset, Paris, 1966.
Pillement, Georges, *Paris Inconnu.* Bernard Grasset, Paris, 1965.
Pitsch, Marguerite, *La Vie Populaire à Paris au dix-huitième Siècle.* Éditions A & J Picard, Paris, 1949.
Polnay, Peter de, *Aspects of Paris.* W. H. Allen, London, 1968.
Reid, Alexander, *Paris.* Phoenix House, London, 1965.
Romains, Jules, *Portrait de Paris.* Librairie Académique Perrin, Paris, 1951.
Rossiter, Stuart, *The Blue Guide to Paris.* Ernest Benn, London, 1968.
Rudé, George, *Paris and London in the 18th Century.* Collins, London, 1970.
Rudorff, Raymond, *Belle Époque.* Hamish Hamilton, London, 1972.
Saalman, Howard, *Haussmann: Paris Transformed.* George Braziller, New York, 1971.
Saint-Girons, Simone, *Les Halles—Guide historique et pratique.* Hachette, Paris, 1971.
Salvadori, Renzo, *101 Buildings to see in Paris.* Canal Books, Venice, 1972.
Temko, Allan, *Notre-Dame of Paris.* Viking Press, New York, 1963.
Vinding, Diana, *Paris in Colour.* Geographia Limited, London, 1970.
Yonnet, Jacques, *Enchantements sur Paris.* Donoel, Paris, 1966.

Acknowledgements

The author, photographer and editors wish to thank the following for their valuable assistance:

The John Allwood International Exhibition Collection, Sevenoaks, Kent; Félix Benoist, Les Anges, Paris; Alain Bernardin, Crazy Horse Saloon, Paris; Julien Besançon, Paris; Paul Bocuse, Collonges-au-Mont d'Or, Rhône; Michel Branly, Paris; Monsieur Bucher, Brasserie Flo, Paris; Cabinet des Estampes, Bibliothèque Nationale, Paris; Monsieur Y. Chausse, Paris; Professor Richard Cobb, Oxford; Yella Daher, Paris; Loomis Dean, Paris; Charles Dettmer, Thames Ditton, Surrey; Jean Didier, Neuilly-sur-Seine; Bernard Dillee, Paris; Indji Dumont, Paris; Wallis Franken, Paris; Christine Gintz, Paris; Bernard Gourgaud, Paris; René Grog, Paris; Anne de Henning, Paris; Madame de Henning, Paris; Hunting Surveys Ltd., London; Catherine Innocenti, Paris; Institut Français du Royaume-Uni, London; Professor Charles Krance, Chicago; René Lasserre, Paris; Gilbert Le Coze, Le Bernardin, Paris; Renée Le Glas, Boulogne; Michèle Leyton, Commissariat Général au Tourisme, Paris; John Man, Oxford; Jackie Matthews. London; Bernard de Montgolfier, Musée Carnavalet, Paris; Nilofar Mosaven, Paris; Musée Carnavalet, Paris; Raymond Oliver, Le Grand Véfour, Paris; Jean Pasqualini, Le Kremlin-Bicêtre, Paris; M. et Mme Hubert Pictet, Paris; Madame Fernand Point, Vienne, Isère; Anna Pugh, London; Christine Schnitzer, Paris; Guy Schoeller, Paris; Hélène Stremooukhoff, Paris; Monsieur Thicoipe, Gardien de Notre-Dame, Paris; La Tour d'Argent, Paris; Shizuo Tsuji, École Technique Hôtelière Tsuji, Osaka; Madame H. Tubiana, Paris; Marie Claude Tubiana, Paris; Nadine Zuber, Paris.

Index

Numerals in italics indicate a photograph or drawing of the subject mentioned.

Colour reproduction by Arnoldo Mondadori, Verona.
Filmsetting by C. E. Dawkins (Typesetters) Ltd., London, SE1 1UN.
Printed and bound in Italy by Arnoldo Mondadori, Verona.